The Preppers Survival Handbook

Step By Step Guide to Become Completely Self Sufficient and Survive any Disaster

Tony Jones

Introduction

Regardless of where you live in the world, you must learn how to take care of yourself. I don't just mean financially. I am talking about remaining safe and secure when the rest of the world is collapsing. Although we learned a lot from the Covid-19 pandemic, it is unlikely to be the least of our worries as time goes by.

One of the most challenging aspects of dealing with a crisis is having the proper mindset. If you understand that there are basic steps that need to be taken, and an idea of what needs to be done, it will be much easier for you to deal with this process. You might not know where to start or what you should do, but it will be easier to figure out the specific steps if you have a plan in mind.

By living a lifestyle where you are always prepared for the worst possible outcome, you will ensure you and your family's safety. And even if the world doesn't collapse around your ears, what do you have to lose by learning new skills that could save a life? The prepper lifestyle can be tough to get used to, but you will have the ability to survive far better than those that assume everything will work out in the end.

Surviving off-the-grid is a major step for anyone who wants to be truly self sufficient. This book will explain why choosing to go off-grid and the steps needed to live like this comfortably.

 It will also help you better understand how to exist in this world without constantly relying on society's support systems.

What Is Self-Sufficiency?

Self-sufficiency is simply defined as independence or an ability to provide for oneself, and is used to describe someone who can provide for all of their needs without relying on others. This is possible to achieve in some cases, but often it's just not practical. A good example would be growing your food. You can plant a garden and grow vegetables or even raise livestock such as chickens for eggs and goats for milk, but providing all of your groceries from this homegrown produce is going to be very difficult, not to mention timeconsuming. Many people do this successfully to supplement their grocery needs, but it is not the only way to achieve self-sufficiency.

Self-sufficiency is often associated with concepts like sustainability and offgrid living. It's not just providing for your survival but also providing resources to be self-reliant and healthy. Self-sufficiency is a great goal to work towards because it means you are improving the quality of life for yourself and others around you. With this new lifestyle, there are often positive health effects, environmental benefits, and financial gains that come with it.

Why Do People Choose to Be Self-Sufficient?

There are many reasons why one might want to become self-sufficient. The most important reason is that you do not want to be dependent on others, and you would like to ensure that your family has access to the necessities in life, such as food, clothing, and shelter.

The motivation for wanting to be self-sufficient is different for everyone. Some people want to become self-reliant because of fear that another economic collapse or natural disaster could leave them struggling with the loss of their job, the value of their savings/earnings, or even an ill family member. Some people want to be self-sufficient because they believe in the importance of living a sustainable lifestyle, defined as having a moderate impact on the environment and resources available to future generations.

The idea of self-sufficiency includes striving to live a simpler life. This is done by reducing the number of people needed to supply your daily needs, being more efficient with the resources you have, and using fewer or no manmade materials to accomplish tasks. Living in an off-grid house or building structures out of natural materials are examples of steps someone might want to take if they are trying to become more self-sufficient.

The Types of Self-Sufficiencies

You can be self-sufficient in many ways, and there are several different kinds of skills and abilities that can be used to work towards being more so. Selfsufficiency can be achieved in physical, mental, emotional, spiritual, or relational aspects. To attain any or all of them, you should determine which one(s) would benefit you the most.

Physical Self-Sufficiency

Physical self-sufficiency involves taking care of your physical needs. You can achieve this by growing your food, obtaining water, and providing shelter or energy to fulfill your daily living needs. This could also include providing your transportation or manufacturing your tools. The goal is to meet your own physical needs without relying on other people or businesses. It is important to provide for your own needs to help you lead a more independent lifestyle.

Mental Self-Sufficiency

Mental self-sufficiency involves knowledge. This can mean having training or expertise in a particular professional field that you can use to find work if the need arises, but it also means that you can provide for yourself in less obvious ways. For example, knowing how to cook your food using recipes and techniques is knowledge, but it's not necessarily a specific skill.

Mental self-sufficiency means being able to take care of all of your intellectual needs without outside help. This would include self-education, learning a skill, solving problems independently, or teaching others to support their growth in knowledge in some way.

Emotional Self-Sufficiency

Managing your own emotions without needing someone else to do it is an important form of self-sufficiency. Emotions can be difficult to deal with and even more difficult to manage. However, people who maintain emotional self-sufficiency can have positive relationships with others. They don't rely on others to cheer them up when they're sad, calm them down when they're angry, or suggest ways to solve their problems when they feel overwhelmed.

To have emotional self-sufficiency, you would need to be able to identify your emotions and know what is causing them. You would also need to be able to communicate these emotions healthily with people who are important to you. It is important to handle situations that cause strong emotions without becoming overwhelmed or stressed out by the challenges that come with them.

Spiritual Self-Sufficiency

Being spiritually self-sufficient is a controversial goal, but it can be beneficial to some people. It involves having faith in something that provides meaning or purpose in your life or fighting for what you believe in. This idea could also include trying to find peace and contentment in what you have or accepting that life is short and should be enjoyed.

You have your values and beliefs, making you spiritually self-sufficient. You have a strong sense of who you are and what is important to you, so there's no need for someone else to be in control or provide direction for your life. It's possible to find meaning in your life without spirituality, but that doesn't mean you should ignore the importance or potential benefits of having something that makes your daily activities purposeful.

Relational Self-Sufficiency

Relational self-sufficiency can be thought of as being able to care for your loved ones, even if they are sick or sad. It means supporting others emotionally while not letting how other people feel affect how you feel. This type of self-sufficiency means that you can still be a good friend, lover, and family member even if you are experiencing hardship yourself.

Achieving relational self-sufficiency means you can separate your emotions from the feelings of others. This does not mean that you don't care about things that other people care about. It just means that you do not allow yourself to be affected by their emotions or feelings.

Financial Self-Sufficiency

Being financially self-sufficient means having enough money saved up so you don't have to rely on others for necessities. It doesn't necessarily mean having a lot of money, but it is about comfortably covering your living expenses for one year without needing to make any income.

Some people choose to be financially self-reliant to ensure that they will always have a safety net to fall back on in case something goes wrong. It's a way of having a plan if you can't work for some reason or if your savings are depleted due to an unexpected expense. Having the money available also means that you wouldn't have to rely on someone else to care for you if you find yourself in debt or unable to provide for yourself.

Right Time to Become Self-Sufficient?

There are a lot of factors that should be considered before deciding to become self-sufficient. First and foremost, you should have a solid support structure around you. If the only person you know is your neighbor down the street, it's probably not worth trying to go off on your own just to become selfsufficient.

If you are thinking about getting your own place, it may be beneficial to have someone with you to help you get settled in or lend a hand when necessary. You should also consider your finances before moving out on your own. It's not always easy being financially self-sufficient, even if you have a plan.

Many people choose to live alone, away from their parent's protection and to experience the real world for themselves. This is often done without considering the potential advantages of having someone around who can help you or provide for you if necessary. If it's not possible to find this support system, it might be better to consider other options.

The more self-sufficient you are, the more you will find yourself on yours. This might make it easier to feel comfortable with being alone or enjoying some time by yourself, but it also means that you don't have anyone around if you need them. If you decide to become completely self-sufficient, you might find it difficult to ask for help even if you need it.

What Is Sustainable Living?

Sustainable living is a way of life that focuses on making decisions that will benefit the environment and ensure that we have enough resources to meet demand. This often comes in the form of conservation, such as recycling and using renewable energy sources instead of non-renewables like oil or coal.

Living sustainably means minimizing your impact on the environment by using things sparingly and not creating too much waste. It might include growing your food instead of buying things from the supermarket to reduce the amount of packaging that comes with it or finding alternative energy sources like solar panels or geothermal heating for your home.

Sustainable living is about finding a balance between enjoying life and ensuring that life will be enjoyable in the future. It means knowing when to put your desire to live comfortably aside and make choices that might not benefit you but could benefit society as a whole.

Why Do People Choose to Be Sustainable?

Most people who choose sustainable living do it because they don't want to contribute to the depletion of natural resources. They recognize that we only have a certain supply of things like oil and coal, and they don't want to do anything that could lead to them becoming depleted sooner than expected.

Sustainable living also means having a smaller impact on the environment. It's about leaving a small footprint instead of making choices that will put society as a whole at risk of depleting resources faster than they can be replenished.

People choose to live more sustainably for many reasons, but it often comes down to living more ethically and doing what we believe is morally right. Sustainable living is about making sure that we look after ourselves and our families, everyone around us, society in general, and the future.

Self-Sufficiency and Sustainable Living

Many people who choose sustainable living are also interested in selfsufficiency. They believe that to live sustainably, they need to be independent of society and reduce their reliance on what others give them. Living this way could mean growing your food, so you don't have to rely on supermarkets for it or generating your power instead of using the power that private entities or the government generate.

Living sustainably and becoming self-sufficient often go hand in hand. They can even help each other along. For example, growing your food ensures that you always have something to eat no matter what happens, but it also reduces the amount of packaging that comes with it. This might be helpful if you want to reduce the waste you produce because you'll already be reducing it at its source.

The difference between self-sufficiency and sustainable living is that one focuses on the individual while the other focuses on the group. Selfsufficiency might mean growing your food or using alternative forms of energy, but it's usually done with just yourself in mind. Sustainable living, however, focuses on everyone around you and how their choices could affect the rest of society.

Self-Sufficiency and the Future

Regardless of your reasons for wanting to be self-sufficient or live sustainably, it's important not to lose sight of the future and everything that might happen because of your choices.

Everything you do has an effect, even if it's just on the environment around you. If many people are self-sufficient or live sustainably, then society as a whole will be affected too.

The future is what you're fighting for when you want to be self-sufficient or sustainable. Even if it's just about being safe and secure in the knowledge that everyone can feed themselves, power their home, and live comfortably, making sure that happens means working together. We might not know what challenges we'll face in the future, but that doesn't mean we should stop trying to do what's right or refuse to make choices that benefit everyone.

Finding Balance

Whether you're self-sufficient and want to live more sustainably because of ethical reasons, environmental reasons, personal gains, or even all of those things combined, it's important to remember that you can't do it all at once.

You'll make mistakes, and sometimes the results of your choices might surprise you.

It's okay for things to not always go as planned when you're trying to live this way because there will be times when sustainability isn't compatible with self-sufficiency. You don't always need to be in perfect balance or make compromises to stay in line with your morals and ethics. Sometimes, the best you can do is keep an eye on everyone around you and try to envision what will happen when you're gone.

It's okay if things aren't always balanced, but we mustn't lose sight of what we're trying to accomplish and where we want to be in the future. Selfsufficiency and sustainable living aren't always compatible, and they can even come into conflict with each other at times. However, there is a balance somewhere in between, and finding it will help everyone involved.

Many people assume that sustainable living and self-sufficiency are either the same thing or that one is better than the other. It's easy to assume that because when you're trying to live more sustainably, this means you are also trying to be as self-sufficient as possible. However, that might not always be true. You might find that you're not self-sufficient at all but can still live more sustainably than others. Or you might be self-sufficient in some ways but not in others. With so many different definitions of what sustainable living and self-sufficiency are, it's safe to say that they don't always go hand in hand with each other.

Environmentalists might want to be as self-sufficient as possible, but that can sometimes conflict with their desire to live more sustainably instead. To reduce waste and do everything they can for the environment, they might feel like they should avoid buying things whenever possible. This means growing their food if they can, even if it's just in their backyard, instead of buying certain foods from supermarkets or restaurants. This might be great if they have the time, money, land, and energy to be self-sufficient. However, there are situations where they should buy things without worrying if something is more sustainable than what they're currently doing. Many farmers are sustainable and self-sufficient, but that doesn't mean that they don't use pesticides or any kind of synthetic fertilizers to grow their crops.

Some people might be willing to trade the idea of being self-sufficient for more sustainability in their lives. Maybe they'll buy food from supermarkets when it's available, even though they know they can grow their own. Or maybe they'll leave for work and come home with food from a restaurant because organic produce just isn't available at their supermarket. They might even choose to live in an apartment instead of buying a house or living on their farmland.

Of course, some people don't care about being self-sufficient at all. They'll take advantage of everything that sustainable living offers, but they won't give up their car or their appliances for more personal gain.

This means that there are different levels of how people can be involved in sustainable living and self-sufficiency, and it also means that these two things aren't always compatible with each other.

Some people choose to try and live as self-sufficient as possible, to support sustainable farming and fight against genetically modified foods. They might only buy organic produce from their local farmers' market, or they might even start growing their food in a community garden or on their land. They might also compost and try to reduce their waste as much as possible, which is important if they want to live more sustainably and help the environment their way.

On the other hand, some people choose to pursue sustainable living even when it means being self-sufficient in some ways but not others. They might buy pesticides to use on their crops, or they might ride their bike instead of walking or driving to work. They'll try to make the best choices for themselves and the environment whenever possible, but there are some situations where they won't worry about being self-sufficient.

Self-sufficiency is the idea that you can provide for yourself without any help from others. This can be in regard to food, shelter, or even money. You don't need to rely on someone else to take care of your needs. There are many ways to become self-sufficient. You can create a sustainable food source, build your own home with the materials you need, or start your own business. The idea of being able to take care of yourself is something that appeals to many people.

The decision to pursue self-sufficiency is personal, but it's also often influenced by environmental concerns. There are many different definitions of what this means for individuals and how they can be involved in sustainable living. Some people might want to do everything that they can to reduce waste, limit their carbon footprint, and live more sustainably with the environment in mind.

Challenges of Being Self-Sufficient

In this modern age, the idea of self-sufficiency is a little out of reach for most people. You might have your farm or garden, but it's likely that you can still go into town in less than an hour if you need to, and the farming and gardening you do aren't enough to meet all your needs. Still, the idea of selfsufficiency is ever-present in our culture, and many people have a dream of being able to provide for themselves.

Self-sufficiency is all about being independent and living without outside help. Self-sufficient people can deal with just about anything that comes their way, from natural disasters to economic collapse. Most preppers plan for the day when everything will fall apart, and they need to fend for themselves.

There are many different aspects of self-sufficiency, none of which make it easy. They range from not buying anything new, including food, to building your own house to essentially living off the land.

Necessity

When the difficult times come, you won't be able to run out and buy anything that you didn't already have stored away. This means planning for every single thing that your family will need: food, clothes, camping gear, tools, and all the little gadgets and supplies that we've come to depend on. And you won't be able to run out and buy new clothes as your family grows, or new dishes as your china gets old, or a bigger refrigerator when you find that you need one.

It's not just about material items either. Sometimes people think that selfsufficiency is about owning a lot of land and raising all your food, but this isn't always the case. You can be self-sufficient in some areas without raising much of anything at all. One way to save money is by buying used items. This can be a challenge in some areas, but it is one of the most important aspects of self-sufficiency if you want to save money and get off the grid.

The first step is to stop buying things you don't need, even though it's not always easy. Most modern people are in debt, not because they want to be, but because some deals seem like a good idea at the time. While you might be able to afford your house payment or car payment, that doesn't mean you can afford everything attached to it. Even if you're not in debt, another important aspect of self-sufficiency is saving money.

Saving money makes you independent because there are enough savings to handle the problem when something breaks or goes wrong without resorting to credit cards or loans.

The Pantry Challenge

One of the biggest challenges to self-sufficiency is planning for every need your family has, which means stocking your pantry and making sure you have what you need from week to week. If the power goes out for a few hours, it's no big deal. If it goes out for days or weeks, you will be in trouble if you don't have any food stored away.

Perishables can be a problem because they go bad, so you need a way to keep them from spoiling. Even if you have a generator to keep your refrigerator running, a lot of food will still go bad because it wasn't stored properly in the first place.

One solution is to use an old-fashioned root cellar, which means digging a hole in the ground that's deep enough so that the temperature is cooler. Some people have already dug their root cellars, but others are forced to buy or rent one. You can also store food in Mason jars with lids on them and then cover the jars with blankets to keep them cool for a few hours until you're ready to eat them.

Another option is to purchase food in bulk that doesn't need refrigeration, such as rice or pasta. You can buy these items in large quantities and stack them in your basement. This will be more expensive than buying a few boxes at a time from the supermarket, but it's cheaper than going without and buying something you didn't save up for when the time comes.

Here are some tips to consider when putting away food:

- Always save up for the things that you need. If it's something that will go bad, then put aside money for it.

- When possible, buy in bulk and don't forget your reusable shopping bags.

- Always buy more than one of anything you might need just in case you use it up.

- Buy from bulk bins, so you don't have to pay for packaging costs.

Laundry Challenges

If you've been taking your laundry to a local laundromat, then you will be in for a big surprise when you try doing it yourself. The first time you wash and dry a load of clothes, it might fluff out to twice the size because of all the water that's left inside the fabric. You may find yourself rewashing clothes to get all of the soap out, but you'll also save money by doing it yourself.

Some people still use laundromats because they've lived this way for so long that it's difficult to change, but if your goal is self-sufficiency, then it may be best to move into a home that already has a washer and dryer. This isn't the only option, though, as you can buy an inexpensive used washer and dryer if you look around.

If you want to be 100 percent self-sufficient, it means going without a dishwasher and doing all your dishes by hand or using paper plates. Some people still use paper plates because they've lived this way for so long that it's difficult to change, but if you don't want to be self-sufficient in this way, then you can look for a home that already has a dishwasher.

The biggest laundry challenge will be washing your clothes in cold water. Most modern washers have a "hot wash" setting that uses a lot of hot water, but you'll have to settle for cold or warm water until you can afford a new machine or find a used one somewhere. On the plus side, buying detergent is cheaper than using the stuff you buy at laundromats because there are no transportation or vending machine costs. You can also save water by buying cold-water detergents, which will be gentler on your clothes and allow you to wash them in cooler water.

Here are some tips to consider when washing clothes:

- When possible, buy laundry items in bulk and don't forget your reusable shopping bags.

- Buy cold water detergents for your washer.

- Do laundry less often since it takes longer to dry things. Instead of every day, try every other day or once a week if you have enough clothes that can last that long.

- Air-dry all your clothes whenever possible. This will allow them to absorb the sun's ultraviolet rays and keep you cooler in hot weather.

Going Green

One of the biggest challenges of being self-sufficient is going green. If you don't care about the environment, this section might not matter that much. If you do, then recycling your garbage will help prevent toxins from seeping into the soil and water supply. You can buy bulk items without worrying about whether they're recyclable or not, but you'll have to learn how to sort recyclables in a bin so that they can be taken to a recycling plant.

You can save a lot on your energy bill by going green. You don't have to install solar panels on the roof of your home. This would be expensive and might take a few years before you start seeing real savings on your monthly bills. Instead, you can put up some insulation and weather stripping around the doors and windows of your home, turn your thermostat down to 65 degrees Fahrenheit in the wintertime, and put solar screens on your southfacing windows.

If your goal is to go as green as possible, you should plant trees in your yard that will help provide shade for your home during the hot summer months. For wintertime, plant evergreens that can be trimmed into Christmas trees or used as firewood when you need extra warmth in your home. The best part about being self-sufficient is the thrill of doing it all yourself.

Here are some tips on going green for self-sufficiency:

- Grow vegetables and herbs for personal use.

- Unplug electrical appliances when not in use.

- Replace cleaning supplies that have harsh chemicals with homemade ones.

- Learn more about composting and incorporate it into your daily life.

The Challenges of Sleeping, Cooking and Eating at Home

Many people don't realize how much money they spend on food until they start making their meals at home. Even if you have a tight budget, you can usually find some money to buy bread and milk for breakfast or lunch sandwiches. You'll save so much money by buying in bulk that it's worth the time spent shopping even with all the walking from the car to the store and back again.

You might think that you'll need a lot of cooking equipment, but all you need is a cutting board, knife, stovetop, oven, and pot for boiling pasta or rice. You can save on water by washing your dishes by hand rather than using a dishwasher because it takes a lot of water to get a dishwasher going. If you have a big family, buying in bulk will help you save a substantial amount of money. You can shop around for various items at various stores. A microwave is useful if you don't have access to a stovetop or oven. You can find them cheap at thrift stores.

When it comes to sleeping, you don't even need a bed frame. If you have an inflatable mattress, then this will help save space in your home. Otherwise, you can use cinder blocks to hold up your bed and put plywood on top for a mattress or memory foam pad if your budget allows it. A simple comforter with two sheets, a couple of pillows, and a duvet cover are all you need for a bedroom.

Here are some suggestions for cooking and eating at home:

- Learn to cook with a cast-iron skillet.

- Compost food scraps.

- Eat locally.

- Grow your food to be as self-sufficient as possible.

Fill a large freezer bag a third of the way with water before closing it, then freeze it for later use as ice cubes in your cooler. This will help keep your food cold longer when you're out camping.

- Cook big batches of your favorite meals so you can freeze them for later use. Just make sure to label the dish with the date and what's in it, so you remember what it is later.

Keeping Up with Modern Technology

You might want to give up on technology entirely once you start becoming self-sufficient so that you have fewer things that can break down and need repair, but this might be a mistake. You will need to keep up with technology so that you can stay in touch with your friends and family and be able to find where you are going if the battery on your GPS dies. This means buying car chargers for your cellphones or having an extra phone charger that works for all of your devices.

Keeping up with the latest technology is challenging for some people, so here are some tips to help you out:

- You can subscribe to online streaming platforms if you don't want to buy DVDs.

- Use your smartphone as a GPS when walking around town to avoid running out of battery power.

- Invest in a good solar-powered phone charger.

- Buy online when it's cheaper, then pick up your order in the store to save on shipping costs.

- You can also buy used items at thrift stores if you're not picky about whether they're working or not. Buying used gadgets can be much more affordable than buying new ones.

Challenges with Transportation

Of course, you might not live in a place where it's easy to get around without your own transportation. This means that you will need to use public transportation or push for better public transit options in your community. Otherwise, you could walk or ride a bicycle everywhere if the weather is nice enough. Carpooling with friends and family can help you save money on gas and save you from having to buy a car. You can also sell your car and put the money towards a more useful form of transportation such as a cargo bike, ebike, or moped.

If you own a car, you will need to save up money to afford to fix or maintain your car. This means buying the correct parts, taking the time to find a good mechanic, and driving more slowly so that your car lasts longer. You might also have to save up for things like insurance if it's required in your area.

Transportation is one of the most difficult things to handle if you're selfsufficient because it can be very expensive. Here are some tips for reducing your transportation costs:

- Ride a bike or walk everywhere if possible. You can also use public transportation.

- Carpool with friends and family, when possible, especially if they live in the same direction as you.

- Only buy a new car if it's a good fit for your budget and lifestyle. If not, look into buying second-hand instead.

- Drive more slowly, economically, and carefully to get the most out of your car.

- Take care of issues like oil changes and tire rotations yourself, or find a good mechanic that's affordable.

- Look into buying a moped or e-bike so that you can save gas, get around easily, and stay healthy.

Other Challenges with Self-Sufficiency

Living in an Apartment

Self-sufficiency is all about doing what works best for your lifestyle, but this might cause some problems. For example, living in an apartment complex might mean that you don't have access to a backyard garden, rooftop garden, or yard, so there are limits on how much food you can grow yourself. You may also have trouble finding animals in your community, or you may have trouble finding community members to help out if something goes wrong.

While it's true that self-sufficiency is all about making the lifestyle work no matter what, not having a garden can be disappointing for those who want to grow their own produce and save money on groceries. Here are some tips for living in an apartment or small space:

- Start by buying a plant that will survive without a lot of sunlight or one that can grow indoors.

- You can also try an indoor vertical garden if you have enough height in your apartment.

- Look into joining a community garden with other apartment dwellers so that everyone has access to more gardening space.

- If possible, find out if your apartment complex will allow you to keep chickens or bees.

- Look into joining a community-supported agriculture program so that you can get products delivered to your doorstep at a reasonable price.

- If all else fails, talk to local grocery stores about any deals they have for getting food waste from their store. You might be able to take the food waste home with you for free.

Living Alone

Another aspect of self-sufficiency that might be difficult is dealing with homesickness, loneliness, or boredom when you're on your own. Working from home can introduce some of these problems because you are at home all day, and it can be difficult to get anything done. When you're self-sufficient, this means that you have to learn how to spend your time productively without going crazy from boredom.

If you live alone or far away from anyone else you know, then life becomes a bit more challenging. Here are some tips for dealing with homesickness, loneliness, and boredom:

- It's easy to get lonely when you're living off-the-grid because you're doing everything all by yourself. Try joining a local club or organization to meet people in your community.

- Stay busy and find ways to entertain yourself during the day when it's just you in the house. You can also organize an online business so that you have the opportunity to work with others.

- You can use isolation as a chance to focus on your plans and goals, making this time more productive instead of wasted.

- If you're feeling homesick, send a postcard to someone that you

  know.

Living in an Underdeveloped Country

Self-sufficiency is hard everywhere, but it's especially difficult in underdeveloped countries where the infrastructure and resources aren't as reliable or accessible. Here are some tips for living in an underdeveloped country:

- If you live in an underdeveloped country, you need to make sure that your home is built to survive natural disasters. Do not depend on the government to do this for you. Also, plan out what you will do if there's a power outage or shutdowns of other services like water supply and public transportation.

- You should prioritize self-sufficiency so that you have the tools and resources to survive a crisis. The more prepared you are, the better chance you have of dealing with any issues that come up.

Regardless of where you live, self-sufficiency is an important part of living a simple life. It becomes even more challenging when you're in a small space or far away from community members who can help out during emergencies. However, self-sufficiency is all about making the lifestyle work no matter what.

If you don't have a garden to grow your produce, find out if there are any community gardens in your area. You can also get involved with a community-supported agriculture program. Also, make sure that you are taking care of yourself during difficult times because self-sufficiency is about relying on yourself when you need to.

How to Get Started

Have you ever stood in a cotton field and watched a honey bee gather nectar from the flowers? Or have you seen a bumblebee carry pollen back to the beehive? If so, have you wondered how these bees can know what they know about foraging for food and then taking it home? As with anything that we humans do, there is always a process behind it. However, for most humans, this process does not happen naturally. It takes conscious thinking and decision-making to accomplish the tasks we take for granted, like putting on our clothes each morning or getting into a car and driving to work.

There is a process that you can follow for achieving self-sufficiency too. In the case of this process, it is a combination of skills and knowledge. To be truly self-sufficient, you need to know how to do everything you need or want to accomplish yourself without help from others. Self-sufficiency isn't just a matter of providing food, water, and shelter for yourself. It's also about being able to do repairs on your home, growing your food in a garden, raising sheep so that you can have your very own wool sweaters, and knowing how to cook from scratch instead of stopping by a convenient fast-food restaurant.

You need to take the time and have the desire to look for the information you need. Self-sufficiency isn't supposed to be easy or convenient. If it is, then you aren't selfsufficient, are you?

Determine What You Need to Become Self-Sufficient

To be self-sufficient, you must first determine what you need to do or have to accomplish your goal. This is the part of being self-sufficient that most people have a hard time with because it requires a lot of thinking, planning, and effort. For example, if you don't have electricity in your home, you will need to either build an off-grid electrical system from solar panels or wind turbines or move somewhere where there is already grid power that you can tap into. If you don't have a well for your water, you will need to dig one yourself or install a rainwater catchment tank. If you need food, but don't have space or money for a garden, then you may want to look into buying bulk seeds and storing them for later use.

Being self-sufficient is all about doing for yourself instead of relying on other people. Many modern conveniences that we take for granted can be easily replicated with a little bit of creativity, effort, and time. For example, you may need to start growing your vegetables in the garden if you don't have ready access to farmers' markets and grocery stores. This will give you the convenience of eating from your garden, but it won't necessarily make you self-sufficient. If everything that you need or want comes from outside sources, then you cannot depend on those sources for things that may be broken or out of stock at the time. For example, if you depend on the local grocery store for everything you eat, what will happen if the truck stops coming one day? The answer is simple. You'll go hungry.

The first step is figuring out what you wish to do and what your goals are. Once you have a goal, you can develop a plan of action. This is difficult for many people who want to become self-sufficient but have no idea where or how to start. You can do things yourself, but you'll need to learn some basic skills. If you don't have the time or patience to teach yourself, then consider taking classes at a local college or school that teaches these types of skills.

To be truly self-sufficient, certain things will need to be part of your plans and goals. One major thing is having an alternative source of power that can adequately meet your needs. All of these things (electricity, gas, oil, wood, and water) need a backup supply in case they are disrupted or unavailable for some reason. Your backup supply can be as simple as having a hand pump for water or a propane gas supply for cooking. Many people have solar panels, wind turbines, or water wheels to provide their power because it is inexpensive and relatively easy to set up.

Think About the Basics

An important thing to think about is how you are going to get the things that you need. This includes food, water, fuel, and shelter. If you live in an area where growing your food will be difficult or impossible due to the climate, start thinking about moving somewhere better suited for farming if it's something that you are passionate about. Many people have gardens for growing food, but they do not live in climates conducive to gardening all year round. This means that the same winter freeze that kills off your garden could also kill you if you depend on your garden for everything. If this is the case, then learning how to preserve food through canning or smoking will be extremely important. If you live in an area where hunting is allowed, then learning how to hunt and gut a deer will also give you something to fall back on if needed.

Water, like power, is another commodity that people often take for granted until they can't get them anymore. Wells needs water to pump, and if you are relying on rainwater to water your garden or crops, what happens when it doesn't rain for a long time? You'll need a backup source of water. This can be another well further down the hill from your house, but this well needs power to get the water up. You could also rely on a water-wheel to get the water up to your house, but this means that you'll need power. If you don't have power yet, and no one is bringing in fresh trucks of water every day, then it's time for some serious planning and problem-solving.

Getting enough food and clean water can be an issue when trying to rely on yourself for everything you need. This is where a first-aid kit, basic medicines, and a first-aid class will come in handy. These should be attended to as soon as possible to make sure you know how to take care of injuries after an accident or another event occurs. Many classes are available through the Boy Scouts, churches, and other organizations that can teach you about first-aid. If having the supplies isn't enough to get you interested in learning these skills, then think about how much it will cost you to keep making trips to the doctor when there is no one else around for miles.

What Will You Eat?

You can learn how to preserve food with canning, pickling, smoking, and drying. Having the supplies on hand will be important if you are trying to live self-sufficiently or if something happens to disrupt your supply lines. You won't be able to just run out for a loaf of bread when you're down to nothing but mayonnaise in your fridge. For this reason, you'll also need to learn how to store food long-term. Canning and pickling will only let you preserve foods for a few months, but smoking meat will let you keep it longer.

Fishing

Fishing is another good way to get the proteins you need without buying fish or meat at the store. You can catch fish with nets, traps, or even with your bare hands. It may take some time to catch enough fish or other seafood to feed yourself and your family every day, though. This is why most people choose to supplement their diets with garden produce when possible. The proteins from animals will give you the most bang for your buck if you're trying to get enough nutrients to stay healthy and alive.

Eggs

Remember that you'll also need fat, vitamins, and carbohydrates, too though. Animal fats can be used to supplement your diet with things like baking, cooking, seasoning food, and so on. Eggs are another good source of protein and fat, but you can also eat the chickens after it's all said and done. Most breeds of chicken will lay eggs every day, and you'll have a constant supply if something happens to one or two hens in your flock.

Fruits, Vegetables, and Whole Grains

You'll also need to supplement your diet with fruits, vegetables, and whole grains. There are many types of fruit trees that you can plant in the ground or containers on patios, decks, balconies, etc. Raised beds are another great way to grow food if you have a yard with good soil or just a patio. Fruits and vegetables will be one of the biggest staples that you need to live selfsufficiently. It's also important to supplement your diet with vitamins and minerals too. This is where a multivitamin will come in handy after a crisis or an apocalyptic event, and we no longer have access to an infinite supply of food from grocery stores, farmers' markets, or restaurants.

It's also important to remember that you'll need other types of food too. Most people like meat at least a few times per week, and it can be expensive to buy even when you go with cheaper cuts like chicken thighs or pork roasts. Growing your vegetables is fine, but most gardens don't produce enough food year-round to meet most people's dietary needs after a major disaster.

Start Small

It's best to start small when learning how to be self-sufficient. You can cut down on your grocery bill by growing your vegetables, but that may not translate into saving money long-term for most people. It does take a lot of time to grow your food, though, and it might not be feasible if you have a full-time job or go to school. In the end, it's up to you to decide what you can and can't do.

You don't need a lot of money either, but learning these skills will take time. Start small with only one or two things you want to learn how to do so that it doesn't feel overwhelming. Once you get the hang of things, you can take on additional skills. You may want to learn how to repair clothes if the only pair of jeans that you have starts wearing out at the knees. That will save you some money since it's cheaper to buy cotton jeans, but still more expensive than homemade ones even though it doesn't cost much to make your own.

Pick a Hobby

Pick a hobby that you love, and you'll learn how to apply it to your selfsufficient lifestyle in no time. You can also teach your whole family how to do the same thing because hobbies are fun too! Gardening is a popular hobby that people love because they learn how to grow their own food, but you can pick anything that interests you. Knitting, sewing, cooking, hunting, fishing, foraging for wild edibles, and making natural medicine are all fun hobbies you can use to save money and become self-sufficient.

<u>Before You Even Get Started!</u>

You'll need some basic supplies to begin learning how to be self-sufficient. Some of these things you may already have at home and don't need to purchase:

Cookware

You'll need some way to prepare and cook your food, and that starts with having good cookware. You can go with cast iron or ceramic pots, but anything safe for the oven, stovetop, or grill will work well too. You'll need at least one large pot, a medium saucepan, and a frying pan. If you have kids in the house, you might want to have them each have their button-up cloth napkin so they can wipe up after eating too.

Water Filter

You can't just drink water straight from the tap without any kind of treatment because there's always chlorine, fluoride, heavy metals, and other chemicals in it that are bad for you. You'll need some way to purify your water at home one way or another. Filtering new water through activated charcoal is an easy option if you don't mind some extra cleanup work. You can buy some buckets and other supplies to make your water filter. Water distillers are more expensive, but they're faster than boiling things on the stovetop or over a fire.

Storage Containers

If you want to store any kind of food, you're going to need some containers. Things like glass jars and stainless steel boxes will keep food fresh for a long time and can be reused repeatedly too. You might not feel up to cooking your beans from dried ones yet, but you should still get some jars or cans so that you can transfer commercially bought items into glass containers over time.

Fire Starter

You'll need a way to start and maintain fires if you want to be self-sufficient. You may eventually get tired of cooking over open flames, but it will still work for some things even after you become more skilled at using alternative ways of cooking your food. Cheap matches are convenient, but they can be expensive in the long run since they don't last long, and you eventually have to buy a lot. For a better alternative, you can use a lighter or any other kind of fire starter instead, such as flint with steel.

Protective Gear

You'll probably be working near a fire, whether you're cooking on an open flame or over a stovetop, so you'll need some protective gear. That means you should do more than just wear cotton clothes if you want to avoid burns and other injuries. Safety glasses, hats, and closed-toe shoes will help a lot. If you have kids in the house, factor their safety into your budget, too, since it's better to be safe than sorry to protect them from dangers while learning how to do something new.

Natural Remedies

There's a good chance that you'll hit some kind of misadventure at some point and end up with an injury or illness. You can't rely on doctors and medications for everything, and they're often expensive, too, so it pays to know how to make your own medicine. If you like baking, you probably already know how to make your care products too. You should also learn how to make some simple herbal remedies and natural first-aid treatments as part of your self-sufficient lifestyle plan.

Plants and Seeds

You're going to need some plants and seeds if you want to start growing your food. Seeds are a lot cheaper in the long run when compared to buying things from grocery stores or farmers' markets. Buying one packet of seeds is enough when starting since most plants will produce an abundance of fruit or vegetables. The same goes for spices, herbs, and other plants. The only downside is that you'll need to wait for them to mature before you can harvest anything.

Outdoor Gear

If you live in an area where the weather's good enough, you'll want some outdoor gear so that your family can work outside even when it isn't time to plant or harvest any crops. Gardening tools, pickaxes, rototillers, and other things are good to have on hand even when you aren't doing any kind of work in your backyard. You should also get some camping gear so that you can scout out new areas.

Solar Panels

You'll need a way to generate power if you want to live off the grid. Many homeowners pay a lot of money to stay on the electrical grid. It can be difficult to get commercial power otherwise, so you should probably go with solar energy if possible. You can also use wind-driven generators or water wheels for some people who live near rivers and other bodies of water. You might not need solar power now, but it's good to know about it since technology is constantly developing new ways of generating renewable energy.

Water Source

You're going to need some way of collecting water if you want to live off the grid. While rainwater collection systems are useful, they won't provide enough drinking water for your family most of the time. There are some really good ways to get fresh water that won't cost you too much money, so invest in something like a rain barrel or water purification system before things get bad. Drinking bottled water every day is expensive so try to avoid doing it, if possible, by setting up your solutions for getting the water you need.

Sewing

If you want to make your clothes, you'll need a way to sew them. You don't have to become an expert at tailoring or anything like that, but knowing how to sew is good for making simple repairs and adding accessories to the few pieces of garment you regularly wear. Many people also use a lot of cloth in the kitchen for cleaning and cooking, so you should pick up a couple of tricks on how to sew since it'll save you money in the long run.

Cooking

You need to know how to cook if you're going to be self-sufficient. There's no reason why everyone has to learn everything, but cooking is one important practical skill that many people overlook. It's easy to go out for fast food or prepare pre-made dishes, but it can be beneficial to learn how to make your meals instead. Of course, the only way you'll know if cooking is something you want to do regularly is by trying it at least once.

Living off-the-grid can be a complicated process, but you should at least know how to make your bread and tea since those are two easy ways of saving money. Learning other skills like herbal remedies, sewing, and cooking will add more value to your life when things start going wrong in your area. You might not need them when everything is fine and dandy, but that could all change in an instant. If you're exposed to the right information and take the right steps, you can start taking back your life today and not tomorrow.

Finding, Gathering and Cleaning Water

Water is one of the essentials of human life, and it is one that many people take for granted. Many people fail to drink enough water when it is readily available, resulting in different kinds of symptoms. However, when one is lost in the wilderness, not drinking water can result in your death within three days (Lin, 2017). Even if you go on a planned hike, there is always a chance that you get turned around and can't find your way back. Although you may have packed enough water for your planned hike, likely, it will not last long. This is why it is so important to know where to find, gather, and clean water to drink.

Finding Water

If you have planned your hike perfectly, you will know where the large catchments of water are (lakes, rivers, etc.). However, you should never drink directly from these sources, as you do not know what microorganisms or pollution may be present. To avoid some dangers, only collect water from fast-flowing water sources found at a higher elevation. This will result in water that has a lower chance of runoff contaminants. Avoid water sources that have an oily sheen as these may contain chemicals that cannot be filtered out or boiled to remove contaminants. It is vital to read your environment. If no plants grow around a water source, or if you note many animal bones, this could indicate pollution. Also, note if there are any mineral deposits around the water's edge. This may indicate highly alkaline-content water, which you shouldn't drink from.

It is also possible to gather water from puddles, especially after it has rained. However, these puddles need to be free from algae and any animal living in it. It will require you to filter and boil it before you can drink it.

Be observant. Plants and animals will also give you clues as to where you can find water. Many herbivorous animals travel along well-established game trails to get to a water supply. You can follow fresh tracks to find their water source. Alternatively, if you stumble across a dry stream, look to where plants such as bulrushes (cattails) grow. They are an indicator of there still being water. You can dig a hole at the base of their roots then wait until the liquid starts to pool before you collect it.

Cattails

Another way to get hydration is to look out for fruit and certain plants known to store water. Cacti, such as prickly pear, have fruit that has high water content. Not only that, but they have fleshy stems with pulp that is edible and have a high content of consumable liquid. However, it's strongly advised that you identify a plant 100% accurately to take advantage of this.

Finding Water in the Desert

There is a much lower chance of finding water in the desert than in jungles and forests. However, that is not to say that you cannot find water if you know what you are looking for. When planning a hike in a desert-like area, you must map out the areas that have known water holes so that you can replenish your water stores as you travel. By knowing the area well, you will also be able to discern where water may gather after it has rained (Protin & Stuart, 2021).

Water will always gather at the lowest point. So if you are looking for water, look in areas at the base of mountains or even in canyons. However, be careful going down into canyons as there is always a risk of flash floods. There is a chance that an area that used to have a river no longer has one, but that doesn't mean that you can't still find water. Areas that appear damp yet have no standing water, places with tall trees or lots of vegetation, and dry river beds are the perfect places to look for water. Start by digging a one-foot by one-foot hole (Bryant, 2021). If the soil remains dry, dig in a different location until you find moist soil (Walter, n.d.). The deeper you dig (either with sticks or a camping spade), the more water will start to fill in the hole. You may have to support the hole's walls to prevent them from collapsing and filling in the hole. The water retrieved from this hole will be dirty with silt, soil, and anything else washed out of the dirt. It will need to be filtered before you drink it. However, if you are desperate for a drink, you can strain the liquid through a shirt to get most of the solid contaminants out of it.

Although some animals are hardier in the desert, they also need to have a drink of water eventually. Know which large animals frequent the area so that you can follow their tracks and find possibly hidden caches of water. Avoid doing this during the hottest parts of the day, as this will only result in you becoming dehydrated and getting sunburned. Even the animals have enough sense only to travel as the weather starts to cool. Insects, such as bees, do not stray far from water. By spotting a swarm of them, you should track where they are getting their water from. Birds are another animal you can follow for water, as they tend to circle over water before getting a drink themselves.

Many people like to assume that you can consume any cactus to get the watery pulp on the inside to quench your thirst. This is a very dangerous assumption. Although most cacti species harbor a large volume of water, they also contain several defenses, such as having a bitter taste or causing stomach issues. Of most of the cacti found in the desert, only the fishhook barrel cactus (Ferocactus wislizeni) is remotely edible with far fewer side effects than other cacti when consumed. And even then, this will not be the most appetizing way to get water. You should drink this in very small amounts.

When all else fails, you can rely on the dew every morning to keep you going until you can find a larger volume of water. To collect the morning dew, you can set out several pieces of cloth over cacti, sticks you have staked into the ground, over rocks, or over trees. The cloth will absorb the water, and you can wring it out before it gets a chance to evaporate with the sun. This cloth can also be used to wipe up any dew which collects on large cacti between the thorns.

Avoid drinking urine at all costs. This is a waste product of your body, and it is being excreted for a reason. It is better to use your urine in combination with a solar still to generate more moisture.

Finding Water in Jungles or Forests

Similarly, as with the desert, you may not find water standing around for you to consume even though there is a lot of greenery. It is because of this greenery that you will be able to collect dew more efficiently. You can lay several pieces of cloth (or t-shirts) to soak up the moisture overnight, and then in the morning, it can be wrung out into a container. Alternatively, when traveling early in the morning, you can tie extra cloth to your legs as you walk through dew-drenched grass to soak up the liquid. However, you need to be sure of the plants you are walking through. The last thing you want to do is drink water that is contaminated with poison ivy.

If you are in an area where bamboo grows freely, you will be able to collect water while you sleep. You will need to bend the bamboo over in an arch, then tie it in place so that the end is about a foot above the ground. Once secured, cut a few inches off the top of it before placing a container under it. The plant will start to leak clear fluid and will continue to do so overnight (Bryant, 2021). Alternatively, you can cut a small hole on the bigger bamboo trees and extract water through a small pipe. This can also be done with plants such as coconut, nipa, and buri palm trees (DNews, 2011a).

Unlike the desert, you are likely to find more fruits and plants to provide you with the liquid you need to prevent dehydration. All the fruits and vegetables that we get in the stores today started from one growing in the wild. Those wild cultivars still exist today, and if you know what you are looking for, you will always have access to not only water but vitamins and minerals.

For this to be successful, you must become well versed in identifying beneficial plants such as wild melons (sometimes known as citrons), squashes, dandelions, wild berries (blueberries, blackberries, raspberries, etc.), aloe (very bitter but edible), and wild mint. You can even use vines that grow among the branches of the trees (Survival Frog, 2016). Be careful when eating too many fruits as this can harm your body, resulting in diarrhea. Green coconuts have a large volume of liquid stored inside of them. However, if you have too much of this, you can give yourself diarrhea, which will add to your dehydration. Unfortunately, not all plant matter is edible, and you will need to do a taste test to see if you can consume what you have found.

If you find a vine, the first thing you must do is make a small cut in it to observe the color of its sap. Any plant that secretes a milky or discolored sap that smells off should be avoided. If the vine has a clear fluid that flows freely, it is likely safe to consume. However, many vines have chemicals on their outer cover, so avoid putting them into your mouth to suck at the moisture. The best way to retrieve this liquid is to first cut the vine free from higher in the tree (about 24 inches up) and then cut away the lower part. By cutting the vine higher upon its length, you prevent the water from pulling away from the cut at the lower end through capillary action. Do not gulp the liquid from a vine! Just because it is considered safer, that doesn't mean that it is completely safe. Allow some of the liquid to rest in your mouth for a few minutes to see if you have any reaction (burning or tasting soapy) before swallowing. If you are overly concerned about a possible allergic reaction, add some of the fluid to the inside of your arm to see if you have any allergic reactions to it.

The roots of plants (ones you know to not be poisonous) also store high volumes of water. You can dig these up and remove a 12-inch section. You can then remove the bark and suck the fluid from it (DNews, 2011a). Alternatively, you can make fine shavings of the root and squeeze the fluid from it. The easiest way to do this is to take a fistful of the shavings, bring it above your head, point your thumb down toward your mouth, and squeeze.

This way, the liquid runs down your thumb directly into your mouth.

Gathering Water

Sometimes, there are visible or even liquid sources of water where you are. When this occurs, you will have to find another way to gather water. When hiking during winter, you will have access to snow and ice. It is never suggested to consume these, as it will lower your body temperature to dangerous levels. You can build a fire which you can use to melt the solid water. If you cannot start a fire, you can collect it in a bottle, which you can place inside your jacket (but not against your skin) to melt it while you continue to look for shelter.

In your hiking kit, you should have some plastic bags, a poncho, or even a tarp, which you can use to collect water. This plastic sheet can be used to collect rainwater or even dew. You can achieve this by tying the corners of your collection material to trees (or having the corners held in place by sturdy rocks (Anderberg, 2021). Add a rock in the center of the collection material to allow the water to gather around it. You will need containers to retrieve the water afterward.

You will not always be lucky enough to have a rainstorm come your way. However, this is not a problem, as you can create your own clean drinking water. Although the water doesn't need to be boiled with this method, it is a good idea to filter it because there is a chance of some solid contaminants getting into the water during the collection. There are two ways that you can "create" your own freshwater.

<u>Method 1</u>

The first is how to get fresh water from saltwater. You can collect saltwater in a pan and bring it to a boil. Once the stream starts to appear, you can add a cloth (or a spare shirt) over the pan. The steam won't contain any of the salt and will condense on the cloth. This cloth can then be wrung out into a container, resulting in fresh, drinkable water (Lin, 2017).

<u>Method 2</u>

Alternatively, you can create a solar still. To make this, you will need a sheet of plastic (six by six feet or make do with what you have), a container to collect water in, several stones and sand, and a lot of green vegetation (Castelo, 2021).

1. Start by digging a hole, preferably four feet by three feet down, though this may be dependent on the soil and the size of the plastic sheeting you have available to you.

2. In the center of the hole, add the water collection container. Around this container, add the vegetation, use as many leaves as possible, and don't allow them to be in the container. This vegetation is what will create the moisture in your still.

3. Next, add the sheet over the hole and place rocks around the edge, keeping the sheet in place. Don't allow the sheet to be taut at this point.

4. Add another rock in the center of the sheet, allowing the edges to slope down at a 45° angle.

5. Now seal the edges with sand of the plastic sheet to prevent any moisture generated from escaping. Ensure that the plastic sheeting will not be disturbed in any way or still will not work. A still works on the principles of evaporation and condensation.

This method works best on sunny and hot days as this will allow the vegetation to produce more water vapor inside the solar still. This vapor will condense against the plastic sheeting. With the sheet angled downward toward the container, the condensation droplets will build before rolling down to collect at the lowest point of the sheet. Once enough has been collected, moisture will drip into the container. Stills should remain sealed for up to 24 hours if you want to get a substantial amount of drinkable water. Alternatively, you can keep a solar still sealed during the day, collect what water was created at night, then reset it for the next day. To collect enough water for your daily needs, you may need to make several solar stills.

This isn't your only way to get fresh water from plants and the sun. Through transpiration, you can use a living tree to generate water for yourself.

-Take several plastic bags that can be sealed, with a small, clean stone inside of them, and tie each one over the
 end of a branch of a tree.

-Be sure to use a tree that you know is safe.

-During the day, the plant undergoes transpiration, creating water vapor inside of the plastic bag.

-The stone inside the bag helps to make a low point that allows the water to gather in.

-When enough liquid has been gathered, remove the plastic bag from the tree and pour its contents into a waiting container. As long as the plant is not poisonous, you can drink this water as is, though it is suggested that you filter and boil it just to be safe.

Cleaning Water

No water supply you come across is going to be completely clean. This is why you should filter and boil any water that you want to drink. Filtering allows you to remove any solid contaminants (Cowan, 2020). Then you will need to boil the water as this will kill the most dangerous microorganisms, such as viruses, bacteria, and parasites (United States Environmental Protection Agency, 2018).

A prepared hiking kit should contain a potable filter or water purification tablets. However, there is always a chance that you may find yourself either lacking these or you may have lost them. Luckily, you can purify drinking water without them.

The first step to cleaning your water is to filter it.

This is generally easier if you have at least two bottles you can use. When you first collect water, and it seems a little cloudy, set the water aside to allow the sediment to settle first.
Scoop any floating debris out and when decanting the liquid, avoid pouring out any sediment that may be resting at the bottom of the container.

While you are waiting for the sediment to settle, start creating your filtration system.

You can create the container out of a large soda bottle with its bottom cut away.

Add some material on the inside of the bottle, such as grass or fine leaves, and insert these closest to the neck. This will prevent the rest of your filtration pieces from falling out of the bottle.

Next, add a layer of charcoal powder. This will help with the removal of many contaminants, fine sediment and will improve the taste. You can create charcoal powder by crushing up charcoal resulting from a fire you have made. You can get away with not using charcoal if you have very fine sand, but it is preferred.

On top of the charcoal powder, add a layer of fine sand, then a layer of coarse sand, followed by small pebbles or gravel. You can even add a layer of grass between the sand and the pebbles if available.

Now you can pour the water you collected through the filtration device. You will need to continually run the same water through the filter until it comes out perfectly clear.

The water may have to pass through the filter several times until this happens. If you do not have any bottles, don't fret.

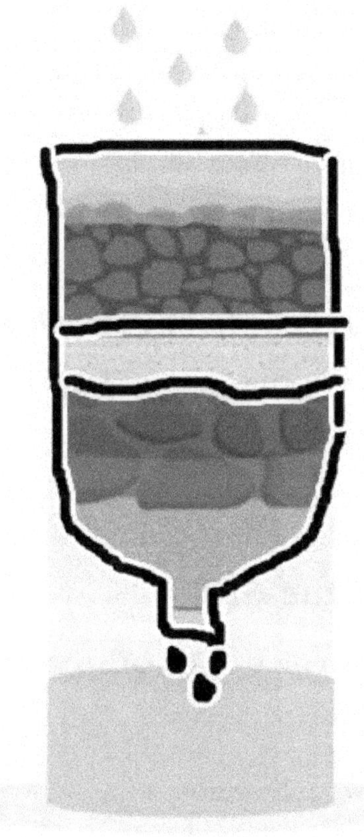

You can use hollowed-out logs or plants such as bamboo to carry and store your water. Make sure that these have been thoroughly rinsed before they are used.

The next step is to get rid of any microorganisms that may still be in the water. To do this, you need to boil the filtered water at a rolling boil for no less than one minute. If you are at an elevation of 5,000 feet or more, you will need to boil the water at this level for at least three minutes.

After boiling the water, allow it to cool naturally before storing it in a clean container that can be sealed or, at the very least, covered

Key Points

Without water, a person will die of dehydration within three days.

If you do not have enough of it, you will need to find more before you become incapacitated from dehydration.

Surviving Off-the-Grid

Have you ever wanted to go off-the-grid, escape society, and live a simple life? Whether it's to get away from the rat race, start a homestead, or whatever else you're running away from, sometimes people want to go offthe-grid.

Off-the-Grid Defined

When you're on the grid, your electricity comes through public power lines, and your phone service comes from a central switching station. When you're off-the-grid, you make your electricity, create your phone network, or find some way to live without tapping into the grid.

There are lots of systems for living off-the-grid, and it depends on what you want to accomplish. Some people will go so far as to live completely off the land. They'll create their energy with solar panels, grow their food in greenhouses, and eat wild game they've hunted themselves. Then some people will make their soap, create their furniture from trees they cut down, and build their own house.

A Life Off-the-Grid

It's easy to romanticize the idea of living off-the-grid, but there are some things you should know before you make that big decision. Here are some important considerations:

Solar Power

If you want to start a homestead, you'll probably need solar power. If you're going to be off-the-grid, then solar, then you have your work cut out for you. It's not the same as just using solar panels to power your laptop. To use it on an industrial level means you need some great skills and thousands of dollars' worth of solar panels.

If you're going to be living off the grid, solar power is a good choice for generating your electricity. You can get large panels that will generate enough power to run all your appliances. You can also get smaller systems to power individual pieces of equipment like a laptop computer or a refrigerator. If you're going to go off-the-grid, then solar power is a good choice. Here are the first steps to getting your very own solar power system:

1. Calculate how much power you will need.

2. Get a list of solar equipment suppliers in your area.

3. Determine how many hours of sun you get per day and what months this is possible.

4. Visit the solar equipment suppliers and ask them for quotes on different packages.

5. Look online for second-hand solar power equipment you can buy at a reduced price.

Depending on how much money you have to spend, you might decide that it makes more sense to hook into the grid system or get other sources like geothermal or wind. You can also buy green energy from your power company. Green energy is usually generated by wind and solar sources, and it may be a better solution than buying the equipment yourself.

Rainwater Collection

If you're going to live off-the-grid, it will be important for your homestead to have a sustainable water supply. If you don't have access to a municipal water supply, rainwater might be the right solution. As with everything else involving living off-the-grid, there are pros and cons. Rainwater is a free source of water, but it may not be safe to drink. It also might not be useful for high-volume uses like laundry and bathing.

Collecting rainwater will require some type of storage, which means using something like a cistern or a tank. You can buy these at most homesteading stores, and they can be made from a variety of materials such as steel or plastic. This is another good reason to go off-the-grid: you'll reduce your impact on the environment by minimizing your use of water storage tanks that are made from petroleum products. Here are some tips for getting started on your rainwater collection project:

1. Decide what type of tank is right for you.

2. Figure out how big your tank needs to be and how much water it has to hold. Be sure to leave room in case of leaks and cracks.

3. Determine where the tank will go. It should be in an unobtrusive spot, far from foot traffic.

4. Make sure that the tank is not in a location that would allow water to run into it when it rains, creating a mosquito problem for your homestead.

5. Buy a tank and assemble it there to save money on delivery fees.

6. Getting the tank properly installed and hooked up with an overflow drain will make it easier for you to maintain your rainwater collection system in the future.

Composting Toilet

A composting toilet is a type of dry toilet that does not flush waste down the drain. Instead, it stores human excrement in an airtight container where microorganisms can break it down over time. This means there will never be any smell coming from your homestead, and you'll have an easy way of getting rid of your waste and making compost.

Although several different types of composting toilets are available, most of them can be broken down into two categories. Passive systems that do not require electricity and electric systems that use fans to dry out the compost and increase the rate at which it breaks down.

The passive system is good for areas where power is hard to get or isn't available in a homestead or cabin. It is also the most affordable option. The electric system will cost more than the passive, but it may be necessary if you don't have a good place to vent your compost outside.

Once you've decided which type of toilet is right for you and installed it in your home, be sure that it gets used often enough to keep the compost from going bad. The composting process works best with daily use, and the average person produces about one-third of a pound of waste each day. It also requires enough oxygen to allow for good decomposition.

Six months after adding human excrement to your composting toilet, you can apply it to your garden as fertilizer. If you want, you can turn it into compost to use in potting soil or to sell at farmers' markets.

Wood-Burning Stove

A wood stove can be a good option for heating your home, and it is one of the most popular backup heat sources in rural areas. In some cases, having a stove will make more sense than installing an alternative heating system. Your decision should factor in how big your house is and how much insulation it has.

Some people avoid wood-burning stoves because they aren't sure about the environmental impact of cutting down trees to make firewood. But it is possible to choose your firewood carefully and give back by planting trees after you've used them for fuel.

You'll find that many companies will try to sell you expensive, high-end wood stoves that aren't very efficient. Stick with low-cost stoves, and don't go for the extra features like blowers that turn it into an air heater. A simple stove with a large surface area will work best, and you may even be able to find one at your local second-hand store for less than $100.

Here are some other options for heating your home without electricity or gas:

Ethanol Heater: This is a family-sized heater that runs on ethanol. A simple outdoor stove can be used indoors in an emergency, and a popular emergency room stove runs on kerosene.

Warm Clothing: Simple things like hats, scarves, and gloves can help keep you warm when it's cold outside.

Fireplace: Open the flue and close off all but one room in your home for heat. You can also use a portable fireplace or wood stove inside if you have enough firewood to last through the night.

Oil Heating System: When your oil tank is empty, you can use the oil from your cars to make it last longer. You'll need about 20 gallons of oil for a medium-sized home.

Growing a Garden

Many people choose to grow produce and raise livestock. This way, they can ensure that all of the food they eat is healthy and chemical-free. Growing what you eat also allows you to supplement your diet with everything from apples and citrus fruit that grew on your land to honey from your beehives.

Even small yards can easily support fruit trees, berry bushes, and nut trees if you have the right conditions. For example, some flowering trees will attract bees that produce honey for you to enjoy. If you don't have space outside, or if buying seeds seems too wasteful to you, consider starting a window farm in your home. You'll be able to add herbs and vegetables throughout the winter without having to go outside.

Here are some other ideas:

Grow Mushrooms: You can grow mushrooms indoors without a lot of effort. You just need the spores, some growing materials like sawdust or straw, and something to put them in.

Container Garden: If you don't have space outdoors for a garden, you can use pots on a windowsill or a patio. You can also use an indoor greenhouse if you want to grow plants throughout the entire year.

Mulching: Mulch your garden with grass clippings, leaves, or straw instead of buying these items from a store.

Raising Animals

There are many benefits to raising livestock. It can be very affordable, and having a small flock of chickens or rabbits is enough to meet most people's meat consumption needs. Some people like the idea of having farm animals over pets because they don't depend on you for their feelings of safety and happiness.

You can keep chickens, rabbits, goats, pigs, and even bees if you have space outside. If you want to raise animals but don't have the space outdoors, consider keeping them in a greenhouse all year-round. That way, you'll be able to harvest eggs from your chickens every day without worrying about predators or inclement weather.

Here are some other ideas:

Keep a Small Stable: You can keep a cow or horse in your backyard if you have the space. They don't need much room, especially if they're outside during the summer months.

Make Cheese: Making cheese doesn't take much time, and you'll be able to enjoy all kinds of dairy products without spending hours at the grocery store.

Keeping Livestock Indoors: If you enjoy the idea of having animals around but don't have space to keep them outside, consider keeping them indoors all year round. You can also use a greenhouse if they don't need as much room.

Making Cleaning Products: Most cleaning supplies come in plastic bottles or cans that can take hundreds of years to biodegrade. Making your cleaners allows you to avoid excess waste, and it saves you money.

Crafting and Repurposing Items

When people are faced with the challenge of living off-the-grid, they quickly realize how many unnecessary items they have in their lives. It's easy to get caught up in consumerism, but when you have to start carrying everything you need with you, it's a lot easier to see what's truly important.

Even if you can't do everything on this list, hopefully, there are at least a few things that will help you out:

Make Your Own Soap: Making soap isn't difficult, and it helps you avoid excess chemicals.

Glass Jars: Many recipes call for glass jars instead of plastic bags. Consider keeping a few reusable containers around so that you don't have to rely on disposable bags.

Keeping a Journal: When your life changes in such a dramatic way, it's helpful to take some time to reflect on it. Keeping a journal can be very rewarding and give you insight into who you are and what you're capable of handling.

Sharing: Consider sharing your skills and items with others in your community instead of keeping them all to yourself. The more we work together, the easier it is for all of us to get by.

Storing Drinking Water

In a survival situation, having enough drinking water can be very difficult. You don't want to rely on the puddles that form when it rains because they don't always provide safe, clean water. If you have a well at your property, you're probably already aware of how deep it is and what kind of soil or rock you're dealing with. If your water is on the hard side or has a high mineral content, consider investing in a reverse osmosis system that's been certified.

If you don't have a well, you can still store drinking water by purchasing large plastic containers from any hardware store. Fill them up at the beginning of every week with clean, potable water, and then leave them inside. Make sure that you have several containers so that you can rotate them regularly.

Efficient Off-Grid Cabin Heating and Cooling

When you're off the grid, heating or cooling your home can be very difficult. You don't have access to the internet, so the best way for you to figure out what's going on outside is by feeling it. If you feel cold air coming through window cracks or if heat is being lost during the winter months, you'll want to make sure that you seal those areas.

If possible, invest in double pane windows, and seal them from the inside with weather stripping or foam insulation. You can also purchase a window A/C unit if your house is large enough.

Another way to keep yourself cool during the summer months is by installing a swamp cooler. Swamp coolers work by using evaporated water to keep your climate manageable. They aren't designed to make the air colder, but they do add moisture and humidity to the air around you.

There are also several small items that you can purchase on Amazon or at your local hardware store for very little money:

Draft Snakes: Draft snakes are foam tubes that you place along the bottom of your doors. They absorb the cold air, insulate your home, and help to maintain a more comfortable temperature.

Window Insulation Kits: These kits are four pieces of clear plastic film that you cut to size and apply to your windows with double-sided tape. They prevent warm or cool air from penetrating the cracks in your windows, and they also protect you from harmful UV rays.

Heat Pumps: These heat pumps are unique because they can work in very cold climates without running continuously. Your home expends very little energy to power the unit, and it doesn't emit a high-pitched noise, so it's great for heating your home at night or when you're away.

Shower Curtain Liner: If there's one thing that this world is lacking, it's good to shower curtain liners. Most of them are poorly made and don't last very long. If you purchase a liner made of plasticized PVC, it can protect your floor and provide some insulation for your showering area while still allowing the water to flow through.

Solar Attic Fans: When you have an attic, it's very difficult to keep your home well ventilated. Solar attic fans are designed to work during the day to pull in cooler air through the attic vents and push it down into your living space. They're also very quiet when they're running. When using them during the summer months, you will have to run them at night if you want to get rid of the accumulated heat.

Radiant Barrier Sheathing: Radiant barrier sheathing covers all of the surfaces in your home, including walls and ceilings, and keeps it relatively cool while still allowing people to feel comfortable. It also deflects up to 97% of the UV rays that come from the sun.

Conserve Power and Water

Most homeowners use an average of 100 gallons of water every day. That seems like a large amount, but using that much water is easier than you think. In many ways, using less water can have a positive impact on your life and your wallet. Just by taking shorter showers or refraining from doing a load of laundry every day, you can reduce your water usage by up to 50%.

If you're worried about not having enough power to keep yourself going during a storm or while you're away from your home, there are several ways that you can ensure that this doesn't happen:

Use Solar-Powered Appliances

Several solar-powered appliances can provide you with the energy that you need to keep your home comfortable while still saving money on your electric bills. Installing battery backups is also an option, but things like portable generators are loud and emit harmful fumes. A solar panel system allows you to produce up to 300 watts of electricity on days when the sun is shining through your window.

Stay Warm

If you're planning to stay at home during a storm or while you're away, use an electric blanket on your bed, make sure that the curtains are closed, and turn on a couple of portable heaters. You could also place some decorative blankets over your windows for insulation purposes.

Save Money on Your Bills

If you've been paying your bills without thinking about them, now would be a good time to look at your budget. You can accomplish this by cutting down on certain expenses or finding ways to make more money. If you still don't have enough money for your electricity bill, consider switching companies or paying in installments instead of all at once.

Surviving off-the-grid is possible, but it requires some serious changes to your lifestyle. It may be simpler and more cost-effective for many people to go with a portable generator during the winter months. However, you'll still want to look into alternative methods of getting what you need out of life without having to pay too much for electricity.

These are just a few of the many ways that you can survive off-the-grid. Knowing what you need and using your resources to their fullest potential is key to ensuring that this lifestyle change goes smoothly. It's also important that you're prepared for things like potential dangers and how to deal with them.

Food and Hunting Animals

Food is another essential item to your survival. However, unlike water, you can last up to three weeks without food, as long as you have water and shelter (Backcountry Chronicles, n.d.). If you are well versed in identifying plants, setting survival snares, and fishing, you are likely going to be fine. However, one of the biggest issues is surviving long enough not to be something else's meal.

Dangerous Animals in North America and How to Handle Them

Many people tend to forget that we do not rank very high on the food chain without our technology, and wild animals will take advantage of that. However, it isn't just predatory animals that can concern someone who is hiking alone or has gotten separated from their group. Some of the most dangerous animals in North America include wolves, coyotes, bears, cougars, snakes, and a menagerie of biting and stinging arthropods (Stinchcombe, 2020).

Wolves

Attacks on humans by wolves are rare, and generally, these animals are skittish. They will likely avoid human contact unless they feel threatened or are protecting a den. Wolves are easy to notice when you know what you are looking for. Their tracks are generally larger than that of a dog with four toe pads and a heel pad. Depending on the soil you find the tracks in, you may or may not see the nail imprints (Carnivora Dinarica, n.d.-b). Their prints measure about five inches long and four inches wide, depending on the species (Washington Department of Fish & Wildlife, n.d.). These are very vocal animals and will communicate with howls when hunting or warning rival wolf packs. They will choose areas with natural shelters, such as rocky outcrops or thick vegetation covering holes close to water to make their dens. This is where the pups will remain until they are ready to join the hunting party. Wolf scat is similar to that of dogs but will contain bone fragments and fur from their prey.

To prevent wolves from coming to you when camping, ensure that you remove all traces of food which can attract wolves to your location. If you come across a lone wolf, as with most large predators, you must remain calm and not run. Running will trigger the wolf's instinct to chase you down. Make yourself noticed by talking calmly and slowly backing away from the vicinity while maintaining eye contact (Carnivora Dinarica, n.d.-a). Under no circumstances should you ever approach a wild animal, especially a predator. Avoid places that are perfect for dens.

If the wolf shows signs of aggression (a tail that is held high, raised hackles, bared fangs, followed by barking or howling), then raise your voice, make yourself appear larger than you are (by opening your jacket), throw items around the animal, and continue to back away (Western Wildlife Outreach, 2012). If the aggressive animal comes toward you, don't be afraid to make use of either bear or pepper spray. Even with all these precautions, there is a chance that you may still be attacked. When this happens, fight back as hard as you can, protecting your throat. You want to make yourself appear as dangerous as possible and not worth the trouble.

Bears

Depending on where you are, you may never see bears, while in other areas, they come strolling right up to your doorstep. They are more common in the backcountry and generally will not bother a human. However, this can change depending on the species and time of the year. It is best to avoid this apex predator as much as possible, so if you plan to be in an area where these animals are, take precautions to keep yourself safe.

A bear has two different-sized tracks. The forefoot track is broader, while the hindfoot looks very similar to a human's shape

(Carnivora Dinarica, n.d.-c). Each foot contains five toes with all claws visible. You will know that a bear is in the region by its droppings and indications of rubbing on trees. The dropping can reach up to three-inch-sized piles that appear segmented. The contents of the dropping can include vegetative matter as well as fur and bones. This will depend on what is readily available to the bear during the season. Feeding areas that have been marked out as the territory of a bear will contain trees that have been used to rub against or be chewed on. Sometimes these trees may also contain fur, which you can use to identify the type of bear species in the area.

The size of the bear's paw prints can help you determine the type of beer in the region and its size (Wildlife Illinois, n.d.). A black bear will have a foreprint of 4–6.3 inches in length by 3.8–5.5 inches in width. The hind print is 6–7 inches in length and 3.5–5.5 inches in width. Brown bears, also known as grizzlies, have fore paw prints of roughly 5.4 inches in width and 5.1 inches in length, while their hind paw prints are 5.4 inches in width and 9.8 inches in length (Hinterland Who's Who, n.d.). Occasionally, a heel print can be found behind the forepaw, showing a large gap between the two pads.

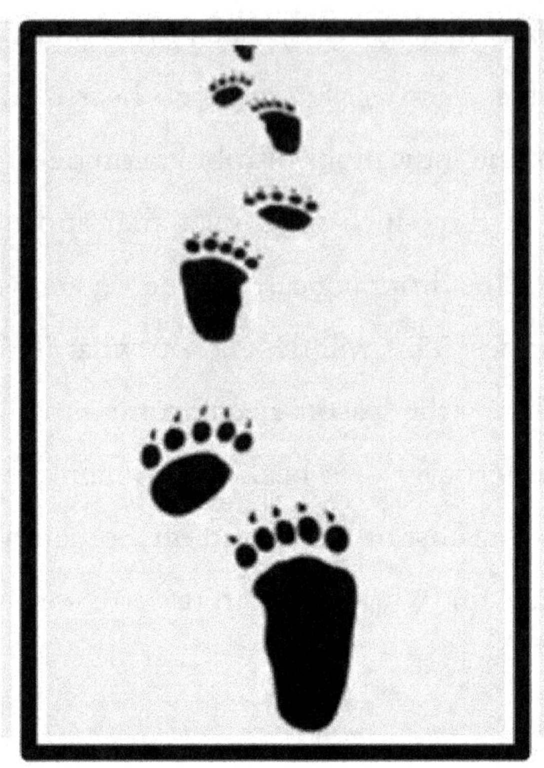

Avoidance is your best bet when it comes to bears. By walking and making noise, such as talking or hitting a stick against the ground, is enough to make most bears wary of your presence. Another safety measure you can take is to remain on the trails and only hike during the day. This makes it easier to see any bears in the region. As with a wolf, if you notice a bear, back away slowly while calmly talking so that you can make the animal aware of your presence and not be startled. A bear may approach out of curiosity. If this occurs, make loud noises, stand taller, and make yourself intimidating. Do not run! Use bear spray if the animal gets too close. These sprays can be up to 90% effective in deterring bears (Miller, 2020).

There is always a chance that the bear feels threatened enough to charge you. When this happens, you need to be sure which bear you are facing, as this can directly impact your survival. If a brown bear were to charge you, it is best to lie down, protecting your head and stomach. The bear will be curious but will likely not continue an attack, leaving you where you lie. You will have to remain lying in this position for 10–20 minutes after the bear leaves to ensure your safety. However, this will not help you if a black bear attacks you. When charged by a black bear, you should do your best to fight back with your walking poles, sticks, or stones lying close by. Continue to be loud in an attempt to scare the animal away. Fighting is the last resort, so be sure never to get yourself into a situation where a bear may charge you (coming between a mama bear and her cubs).

Coyotes

This shy canid is rarely known to attack adult humans but will not turn its nose up at young children or family pets. You are likely to hear coyotes before you see them. They communicate with various vocalizations from barking, yipping, whining, and howling (Urban Coyote Research, n.d.). Their dropping is similar to a dog's but tends to be more rope-like due to the hair and bone fragments that remain. This dropping is also used to mark territory and communicate with other members in the pack. Their tracks are similar to that of dogs, but their four toes tend to point more inward. These tracks are often seen heading in a straight line, whereas a dog's will meader. Their tracks measure two and a half inches long by two inches wide (Washington Department of Fish & Wildlife, n.d.).

Although rarely a threat to adults as they are shy canids, they will not miss an opportunity to take a pet or an unattended young child. The first thing you want to do is avoid baiting these creatures to your camp, so practice camp hygiene. Keep your pet or child close to you. A coyote will try to put itself between you and its prey, preventing you from coming to its rescue (Ackert, 2011). Don't allow this to occur. Pets should always be kept on a leash that doesn't extend beyond six feet, and children should remain at your side at all times. Follow all other large predator rules when you come across a coyote, and remember never to run!

Cougars

Likely you won't even know a cougar is stalking you until it has decided to attack you. They are very stealthy and prefer not to be seen. Although they rarely attack humans, attacks have been known to happen. Cougar tracks are very similar to wolf tracks, especially if you cannot see any claws present as this large cat can retract them. To discern which track belongs to which animal, you will need to look at the heel pad and the toes carefully. The heel pad is divided into three parts, while the toes are teardrop-shaped, with the second toe being the lead toe (Wilderness Arena, 2019). Their prints are roughly 3.5 inches in width and three inches long (Western Wildlife Outreach, n.d.). Similar to bears, this large cat also rubs against trees. However, you are more likely to see scratches on the ground accompanied by sprayed urine. This is to mark the animal's territory. The dropping is made up of blunted segments that are smooth, with a strong odor.

If you manage to startle a cougar, don't approach it any further and follow all the other large predator safety precautions (Path Projects, 2020). If it takes an interest in you, appear threatening by raising your arms above your head and making a lot of noise. You may even have to throw sticks and stones to prevent it from mock charging you. Even if the animal seems to retreat, keep an eye on your surroundings as they are ambush predators. Once they decide to hunt you, it may be difficult to get rid of them.

Use a bear spray to dissuade them from coming close to you if necessary. If a mock charge turns into an attack, defend yourself by aiming for its head as much as possible. Protect your throat and head while you do this to prevent either its teeth or claws from sinking into you.

Snakes

Not all snakes are venomous, but they should be respected, especially if you can't tell them apart. Snakes will never go out of their way to attack a human. Most snake bites occur because a person wasn't paying attention to where they were going or listening for the warning signs that snakes give them. The venom produced is a costly resource for snakes. Therefore, wasting it on an item that it cannot eat could mean the difference between a potential meal or the snake going hungry. There are different snakes in different regions, so be sure to research what is in your area. This way, you can identify and avoid any potentially dangerous snakes.

Different snakes have different ways to move, and you will only be able to notice their tracks in soft soils, sands, mud, or dirt. The most common snake tracks that you will come across are side-winding, concertina, rectilinear, and lateral undulation

(Wildlife Removal, 2019). The size of their droppings can also hint towards the size of the snake you may come across. This oblongshaped dropping tends to be squishy and dark brown when fresh but becomes chalky as it ages. It may also be surrounded by a white puddle of urine, as the same opening excretes both waste products.

Depending on the species, most snakes will warn you of their presence long before you are near them. They will hiss or rattle. This is why it is important to be attentive, especially when collecting firewood or walking around in an area where snakes are most active (UC Davis Health, 2018). Usually, when a snake is encountered, you can stand still, and after some time, the animal will leave the scene. The best way to avoid the dangers of a snake bite is to have the appropriate clothing to protect you from a surprised snake attempting to bite you. This includes sturdy walking shoes or boots, as well as long pants. It is best to remain on the well-traveled trails as you are least likely to encounter a surprised snake.

Never handle a snake that you can't positively identify as non-dangerous, even when the snake appears dead. Playing Dead is a survival instinct for some snakes. However, if they are touched, they will defend themselves with a painful bite that may or may not have poison (a dry bite versus a regular bite). This is why it is important never to wander off alone. By remaining in pair, if something were to happen, you have someone who can give you immediate first aid. If you are by yourself, continue to make as much noise as possible as you move, as this will also alert any snakes to your presence. This will cause them to avoid you.

Ticks

If there are animals, there will be ticks. There are various species of these parasites that cause many different kinds of disease. Some of which will require treatment you will not be able to get while out in the wilderness. The best way to prevent yourself from getting bit by ticks is to use bug repellent and wear the appropriate clothing. As with all parasites, you won't know where the ticks are until you have one on you already. The best way to avoid these critters is to practice prevention.

Always wear socks, shoes, and long pants when hiking, as this will prevent ticks from climbing onto your skin (Ontario Hiking, 2021). To prevent them from crawling up your pants, tuck the pants legs into your socks. For added protection, you can add insect repellants to the cuffs. By wearing lightcolored clothing, you should more easily see ticks crawling on you and thus be able to remove them before they get a chance to bite. Ticks generally like to hide in tall grass and foliage, where their hosts like to walk through. Remain on the trail to avoid picking up extra passengers. To avoid ticks completely, as well as mosquitoes, hike during the colder parts of the year. When a tick does manage to latch itself to you, remove them carefully so as not to leave the head behind, as this can cause infection to occur.

Other Stinging and Biting Arthropods

Throughout most regions of the world, you will find different kinds of scorpions, spiders, bees, wasps, hornets, and others, which can make your hike unpleasant. Except for accidentally stumbling across an arthropod that bites or stings, you will generally remain safe from these animals as they tend to avoid humans. It is a good idea to avoid these creatures when you encounter them. Especially bees that will sting you as a swarm when you disturb the hive.

It is unlikely that you will manage to avoid all insects and other biting and stinging arthropods. Your best bet is to add insect repellent (20–30 % DEET) to your hiking arsenal and cover up the most exposed skin (Densmore, n.d.). This should deal with most blood-feeding insects. Alternatively, if you are settling for the night, aim to burn some cedar or redwood, which has natural insect repellent properties. Avoid areas that have blooming flowers or rotten fruit as this will attract insects such as bees and wasps. When eating any fruit that you forage, be sure to wash your hands to prevent the attraction of insects that like sugary treats. Bright-colored clothing may also turn you into a bulls eye for bees that are looking for flowers. If this does occur, do not hit the bee because this will just cause it to sting. When coming across a hive of stinging insects, slowly back away and don't kill any of the insects that are on you. This can cause you to become marked, and the rest of the hive will come for you.

Some General Rules

These are hardly the only animals that can hurt you. If you want to survive in the wilderness, here are some more general rules that will keep you safe from wild animals.

- Avoid using deodorants or toothpaste with a strong scent, which will attract animals (Kairis, 2017).
- Know which animals will pose the biggest threat if you plan to hike in a specific area, and prepare appropriately.
- Where possible, travel in a group, making as much noise as possible.
- Do not cut your sense of hearing by wearing a headset when hiking (Pennings, 2019).
- Also, use your sense of smell. If something doesn't smell right (animal's natural musk or a rotting carcass), move away from the area.
- Don't hike at night, dusk, or dawn, as this is when predators are on the prowl for prey.
- Stick to walking during the day and camping with a fire at night to keep yourself safe.

Edible Animals

Even though there are animals that would use you like food, there are many others you can use for food. Foraging, trapping, and hunting for animals like a food source can be difficult to do physically and mentally. Many of us have never had to kill an animal for food, but this will be necessary when you are in a survival situation. As long as you can lessen the hunted animal's suffering, the better. Another aspect of hunting for protein is that you may have to resort to a protein you may be disgusted by (such as maggots). Making it not only difficult to handle but also to swallow.

Birds

This is likely not a protein source you will easily catch on your own unless you can identify roosting spots. Depending on the season, you may find birds such as ducks and geese that sit in nests full of eggs (Hunter, 2020). Even if you can't catch the bird, you can use the eggs as a protein and fat replacement. There are many kinds of grouse, quail, partridge, and other large birds that you can attempt to hunt throughout America.

Rodents

Rodents such as mice, rats, squirrels, and chipmunks are usually scarce during daylight, but they move around from dusk to dawn. Although they do not have a lot of meat on them, they are edible after being skinned, gutted, and roasted. These creatures are generally fast, and it may be difficult to catch them by hand. You will need to use traps or snares to catch them.

Rabbits and Hares

These animals are found through most states and in varying concentrations during the year. They contain more meat than what is on the smaller rodents and can be cooked similarly. They tend to be more active during dusk to dawn, with rabbits remaining close to their warrens and hares looking for food close to places where they can run and hide. Snares are your best bet when trying to catch these fleet-footed creatures.

Aquatic Life

Regardless of being close to saltwater or fresh, you will find something to eat either through fishing or foraging around. Although catching fish may be difficult without a rod and hook (although you can make these yourself), there are many ways to catch these animals. Even bullfrogs and snapping turtles are edible if you can catch them by hand. Bullfrogs pose no real threat when caught by hand. However, be careful when catching snapping turtles, as their beaks can easily take a finger or two if you get too close.

Although it is possible to consume salamanders, it is best not to as many species tend to secrete irritating substances through their skin. These creatures also exhibit aposematism, which is a form of protection. Unlike camouflage which causes the animal to remain hidden, aposematism tells predators that the animal exhibits colors such as white, red, orange, black, or yellow that may be poisonous when eaten (Potochny, 2020).

Other aquatic life that you can use as a food source, especially if you find yourself along a coastal area, are crustaceans and shellfish. These creatures can easily be collected in a quantity that keeps you from getting hungry. However, you will need a knife to be able to get most shellfish, such as limpets off the rocks they are on.

Creepy Crawlies

There are 1.1 million insect species currently identified, of which 1,700 are edible (Potochny, 2020). And before you turn your nose up at eating insects, many cultures around the world make use of this high-protein, low-fat food source. Although many creepy crawlies (insects, snails, scorpions, etc.) do not look appetizing, they are edible once cooked. As with the salamanders, insects with warning colors are best avoided. Stick to eating insects that are green or brown. Some insects secrete chemicals to protect themselves from predators, so it is best to avoid them if an insect has a strong odor.

You are spoiled for choice when it comes to choosing what insects to eat. If you have a space, you can dig into termite and ants nests (not fire ants) where you can collect masses of clean protein. If you know-how, you can also smoke out bees from a hive, allowing you to get to the energy-rich grubs (larva) and honey. Large water beetles and June bugs are also edible once thoroughly cooked. Even grasshoppers, crickets, and locusts (if you can catch them) are edible and can be found throughout most of summer and spring. You do not even need to go after the faster creepy crawlies. Turn over rotten logs or rocks to find slugs, cockroaches, centipedes, scorpions, and earwigs. When collecting scorpions, be sure to pin down the tail to prevent the animal from stinging you.

Any creepy crawly you find should never be eaten raw. These creatures may be covered in bacteria or have internal parasites that could make your already dangerous situation more deadly. Either roast or boil what you find before consuming anything, and remember to remove the legs to prevent them from getting stuck in your throat.

Larger prey

The chance of you taking down a deer or moose without a weapon is a fantasy. However, that is not to say that you cannot use this source if you come across it. You may find scraps left behind by predators that you can use. However, taking from a carcass may put you in danger of running into a predator or scavenger. Be sure that the coast is clear before gathering what you need either as food or bait for your traps.

Traps and Snares

Unless you go exploring with a gun or similar weapon with you, you may find that hunting can become difficult as prey is significantly faster than you. However, that is not to say that you will starve. A well-kitted hiking bag should contain all you need to make traps and snares that can provide some source of food if you get lucky. Even if you don't have everything handy, you should fashion the resources you may need. The advantage of setting a trap is that you lower the amount of energy expended by looking for food (McCarthy, 2017). The disadvantage is that they do not always work. Most states do not allow snaring of animals when it comes to hunting. However, if in a survival situation, and it is the only way to get food, you have to use it. That said, make sure that you check your traps and snares at least two to three times a day to ensure the animal you have caught isn't needlessly suffering.

Fish Traps

Unless you are an expert, you may find it difficult to catch fish with your bare hands. Your other options can include fashioning a fishing rod or a spear; even then, these do not guarantee your success, especially if you do not have a bait (Practical Primate,

2018). Two of the easiest fish traps to make are the bottle trap and the funnel trap.

Bottle Trap

To make the bottle trap, you will need one large soda bottles. You will also need some rope or dental floss to keep the bottle sections together.

Start by cutting the top end of bottle (see image).

Cut some small holes in the side. These holes will allow water to flow through the trap once it is set.

Remove the cap from the bottle.

Slide the cut section of the bottle into the first part so that you can thread the cordage, rope, or dental floss through to keep the bottle sections together.

Add a small piece of bait through the opening of the funnel, so that it is lying in the space between the two bottles.

Tie the anchoring line to a sturdy branch that overhangs the slow-flowing river or tie it to a branch that has been hammered into the mud of the river bank. This will prevent your trap from being carried downstream.

You can also stake the trap in place with some sticks. This way, the wider opening of the trap allows the flow of the river through it.

If the trap floats too much, add a small rock to join the bait to help it sink down.

Leave the trap for a few hours.

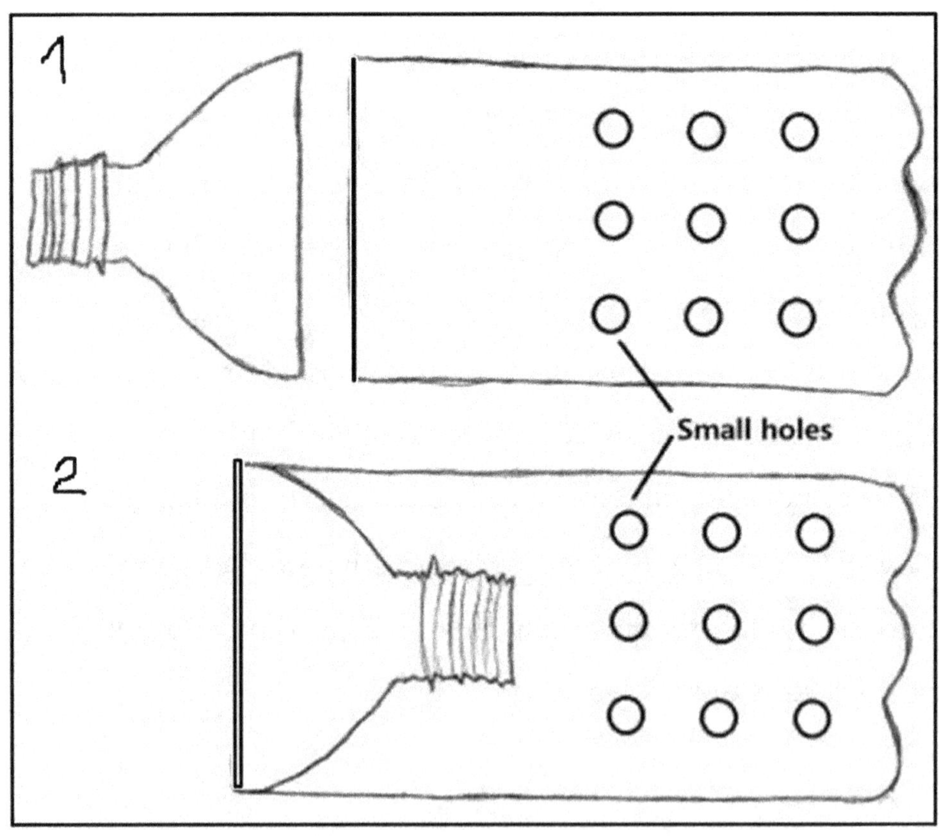

This trap is designed to catch smaller fish which you can use for bait or a quick snack. The fish you catch with this method will not be enough to make a full meal.

M-Shaped Funnel Fish Trap

Start with getting many long sticks which you will use to construct the legs of the M-shaped funnel. Start from the shore and place them close together until the water reaches a depth of halfway up your shin.

Ensure that the sticks stand above the water to prevent fish from jumping over and out of the trap.

Next, build the two shorter legs, which make up the final point in the M-shape, but do not complete it. Leave a small part of the funnel open to allow the preferred-sized fish into the trap. Inside the trap, add water plants found in the area so that the fish have a place to hide and be shaded from aerial predators.

Add bait to the pool and wait for the fish to swim into the trap.

The second trap, the funnel trap, is also known as the M-shaped funnel fish trap (Survival Skills Guide, 2017), and only requires natural resources that you should be able to find in your general vicinity.

As with all traps, this process takes time and may not always be successful. Because of this, don't hedge all your bets on a single trap working. The more you set out, the larger your chance is of catching something.

Animal Traps

Holes

This is one of the most primitive traps and can work well if the
construction prevents the prey item from getting out (McCarthy,

2017). These sorts of traps are great for catching smaller animals such as lizards and rodents.

Start by digging a hole that is about 18 inches deep.

Construct the walls so that they lean inward and not outward. This will make it more difficult for the animal to escape from the hole.

Create a shelter over the hole. By doing this, you create a sheltered spot for a small animal looking for food or trying to escape a predator.

A shelter can be constructed with a large, flat piece of wood or slate, which is placed on top of four small stones or mounds of soil. This will create a gap between the ground and the shelter. You can add some bait to the hole to entice the prey as well.

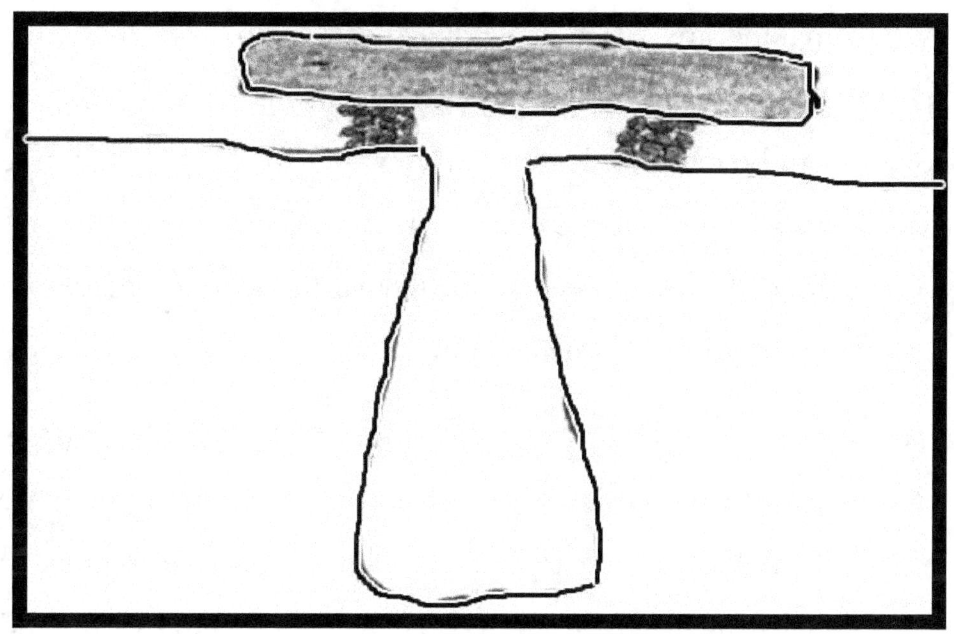

This trap may not always work as the animal may be able to scramble out or jump. If you have a bucket, you can bury it in the hole. With its smooth sides, the prey will struggle to get out.

Snares

When walking around, keep an eye on your surroundings. You may be able to find tracks of rats, squirrels, rabbits, or hares. All of these animals you can catch through the use of snares. The two main forms of snares you can use are the drag or noose snare and the twitch-up snare (McCarthy, 2017).

When making any snare, it is vital that the hole created is big enough to have the prey's head to go through for it to work. Snares can be made with sturdy, thin wire (as with picture frame wire) or malleable cordage that can withstand a struggling animal. You will need about three to four feet of the wire or cordage to make a snare to catch smaller animals.

To create a snare, make a loop at the end of the wire or cordage, and twist or tie it in place. Then thread the other end of the snare through the loop to create a cinch. This is what will tighten as the animal struggles to get out. You can create several snares and carry them with you until you find the perfect place to set them.

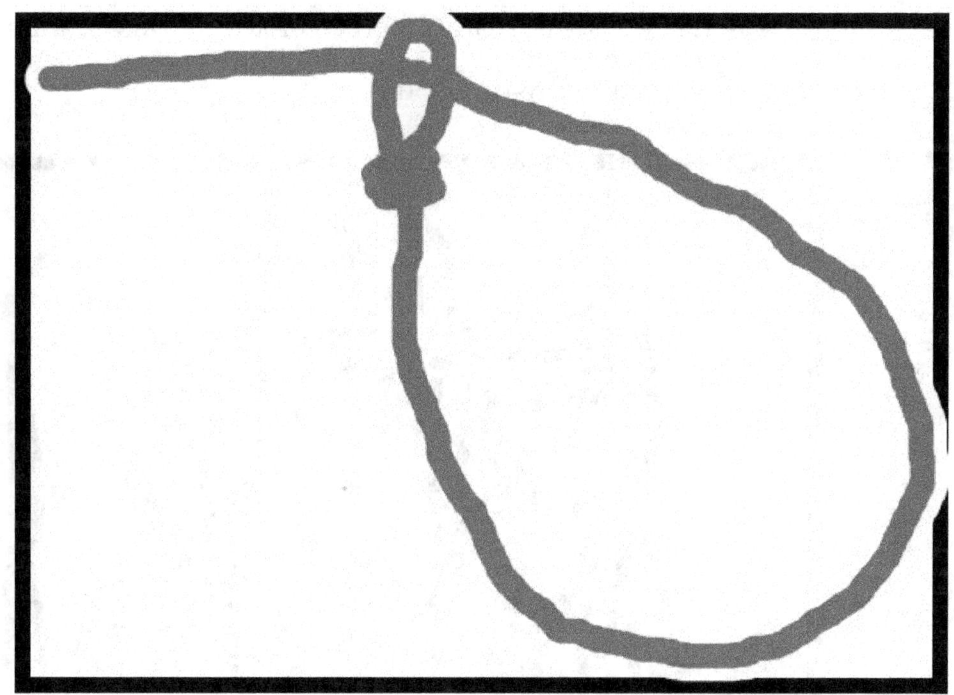

Animals are very particular in the trails they like to travel. Once you find such a trail, determine in which direction the animal was traveling. Then start on creating a funnel. By lining part of the animal's route with closely packed sticks, you can channel it to the area where the snare will be. If a sturdy branch goes horizontally over the funnel you have created, you can tie the snare onto it. Afterward, you can lay the snare across the path the animal is likely to take. Ensure that the snare is firmly tied in place, as you do not want the animal to break the snare loose, only to die later, far away from where you are. If this branch is not available, you can construct one.

Take two sturdy branches that end in a V-shape. Hammer these into the ground so that they cannot be uprooted easily. Then set another branch in the two crooks of the stand before tying the snare to it and setting it. To prevent this horizontal branch from being dislodged, you can also tie it in place. The size of the snare should be roughly the size of your prey's head. Any smaller, it won't catch your intended target, as they will move it out of their way. If the loop is too large, the animal will simply hop through it. These traps can be baited with food that the prey has been eating. Snares need to be checked every couple of hours as dead prey will be snapped up by any predators in the region.

Twitch-up Snare

To avoid a predator from getting to your prey and prevent it from getting away before the snare has a chance to tighten properly, you can make the twitch-up snare.

For this to work, there needs to be sapling close enough to be bent down and kept under tension without breaking.

Next, you will need two pieces of wood, one of which will be the anchor for the trap, and the other will connect into this to keep the sapling under tension.

Create the funnel as previously described. Then create the anchor piece of wood. This should have a notch near the top that matches the notch in the second piece of wood.

Hammer this into the ground close to where you want to set up the snare.

 Ensure that it cannot be pulled from the ground with ease.

You can also hammer the second piece of wood next to this to create a wedge that ensures it stays firmly in the ground.

The second piece of wood will contain both the snare's wire and another wire or rope which will be tied to the tree.

Add the snare wire close to the notch that connects to the anchor. You can carve a divot around the top of it where the second wire will be tied to prevent it from slipping when the tree shoots up.

Bend the sapling over, tie the line to it, then set the trap by connecting the two notches.

Ensure that the snare covers the hole in the funnel so that the animal will be caught in it.

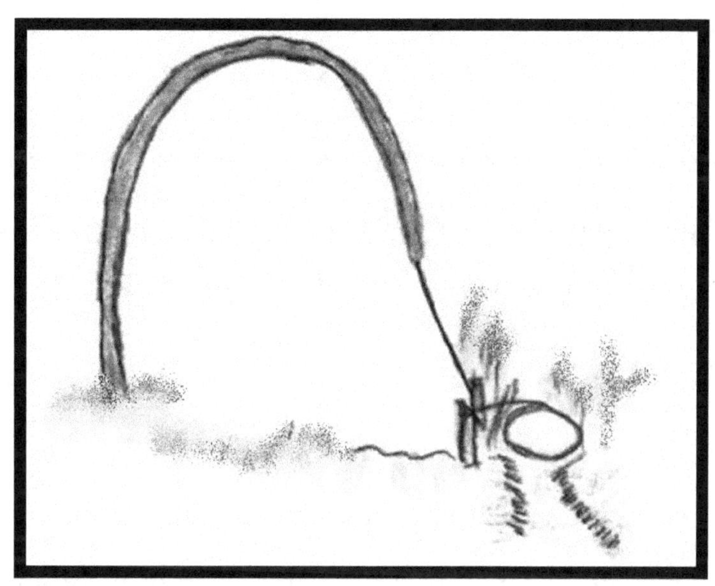

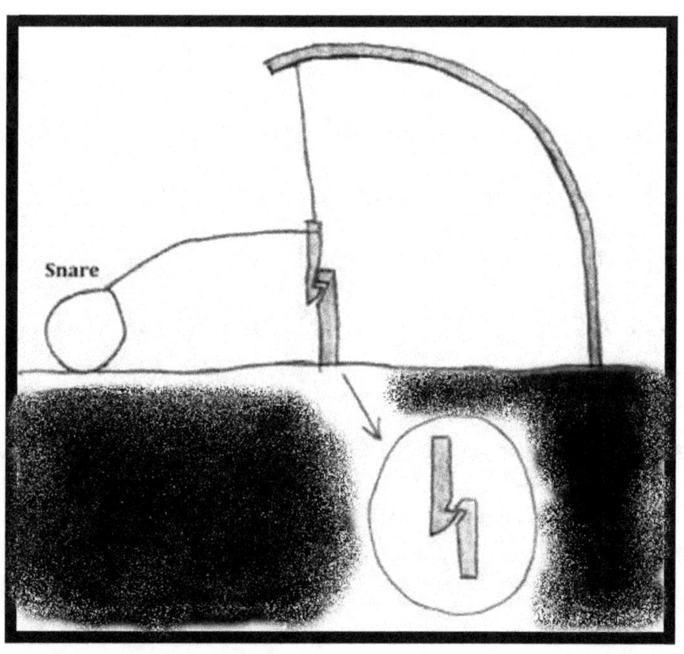
Snare

When this trap is sprung, the animal will be pulled into the air. This causes the cinch to tighten and keep the prey out of land-dwelling predators' maws.

Key Points

Gathering food is a must if you are lost in the wilderness. However, while you are hunting, so are other animals.

Predatory animals are dangerous and should be avoided where possible.

As long as you make a noise while moving, most animals will avoid you.

If you come across a dangerous predator, keep your voice low, keep your eyes on the animals, and slowly back away.

Most predators will not attack you, but if they become inquisitive, become louder, make yourself appear bigger than you are, and throw items.

If an animal becomes aggressive, do not run! This will trigger their hunting instinct, resulting in you becoming prey and not a threat.

When attacked, defend yourself appropriately, depending on the animal attacking you.

Avoidance is better, don't go after an animal you do not intend to hunt and eat.

There are many edible animals in the wild, as long as you aren't too squeamish.

Most insects are easily caught. However, mammals, birds, and fish are more difficult to catch and will require different strategies to obtain them.

Some animals are easier to catch if you use traps or snares, so be sure to keep the necessary equipment on hand.

When using traps or snares, remember to remove or break them down when you leave the area. If you are not hunting the area, there is no reason for it to be left behind to kill needlessly.

Building a Shelter

Shelter is one of the three essentials you will need for your survival. According to the rule of threes, in harsh weather, you will only have three hours in which to find shelter before losing your life (Backcountry Chronicles, n.d.). However, the worse the weather, the less time you will have. How and what kind of shelter you decide to build will depend on shelter size and material used. It also depends if you want to have a shelter that is for long-term survival. The type of shelter you build also needs to reflect the environment that you find yourself in. Some shelters may need some equipment to build, while others can be done with only the resources you have on hand. Review the situation you are in and what is at your disposal to make an educated conclusion on what you need at that moment.

Building Shelter Basics

Regardless of where you are, there are some basic shelter rules to follow. The first thing you need to consider is where you will build your shelter (Vuković, 2020). Look for natural sheltered areas that have a wall of trees or rocks around them. These will add extra protection against wind and driving snow or rain. The area you want to build a shelter in needs to be dry and flat. Don't camp too close to water, especially if it has been raining, as the water level can rise, resulting in your camp getting flooded. You do not want to get wet, as this can compromise your survival. Be wary of anything that could land on your shelter after you build it. This can include dead trees or branches or even rocks if you are close to the bottom of a cliff.

Clear the area of any debris before lining where you will be sleeping, as there could be insects or other nasty crawlers lurking within the debris. Prepare the area with fresh leaves, pine needles, or loose leaves. This will create an insulating layer that will protect you from heat and cold. You will also need to clear an area where you want to build a fire, as you do not want to start a forest fire accidentally. Then lastly, if you are aiming to have someone spot you, you must tie something colorful to your natural shelter. Most built natural shelters tend to camouflage well, making it difficult to spot if rescuers are looking for you. A fluttering piece of bright material attached to or close to your shelter will be eye-catching enough for most people.

Desert Shelter

When in a desert or the area you are hiking in is experiencing a heatwave, the first thing you want to do is find a shaded area. This may be a group of cacti, a rocky outcrop, or, if lucky, some trees. When you find some shade, drink some water before moving on to building your shelter. Some equipment you may need includes a tarp, emergency blanket, poncho (any protective layer), some walking sticks or branches, and something to act as a weight (DNews, 2011b).

Dig a trench, long enough to lie down in. This should be about a foot to two feet in depth. Don't exhaust yourself too much if possible. Create a slope into the trench to make it easier to get in and out of it.

Using branches, walking poles, or even surrounding rock outcrops, lay or tie the protective layer over the top of the trench by about afoot.

If you have enough material left, create a second layer about a foot above the first layer. When using an emergency blanket, turn it so that the silver side is facing out. This makes you more visible and reflects the heat away from you.

By creating these two layers, you can lower the temperature in your trench by 20–40°F.

Although a trench does help to lower your temperature, if the heat is too high, it is best to set up your shelter and wait until it is cooler to dig. Deserts become freezing at night. Because of this, you may have to deconstruct your shelter and wrap it around yourself in a burrito fashion to keep warm in your trench.

If you have many people in your party when lost in the desert, each person will need to construct their own trench shelter. Alternatively, if there are trees and leaves, the group can construct a wickiup (wigwam) or dome shelter. However, this may require more tools and resources that are available to you at the moment.

Snow Shelter

Not everyone expects to run into a sudden snowstorm. If this happens to you and you need to find shelter with no time to build anything, you can construct a tree pit shelter (Sullivan, 2019).

Look for a tree with a dense canopy of branches and dig down at the area around the trunk. This is known as a tree well or a spruce trap.

Be wary of this tree well, as the snow that does get in there is generally not as densely packed as that around it. This can cause you to fall into it and struggle to get out.

Continue to dig down until you manage to reach the ground. While you do this, support and pack the walls around you to prevent them from collapsing inward.

Take some of the branches that you can reach and lay down a layer on the ground. This should be about six inches thick to protect you from the cold.

Some more branches can be added over the top of the shelter to protect you from the wind.

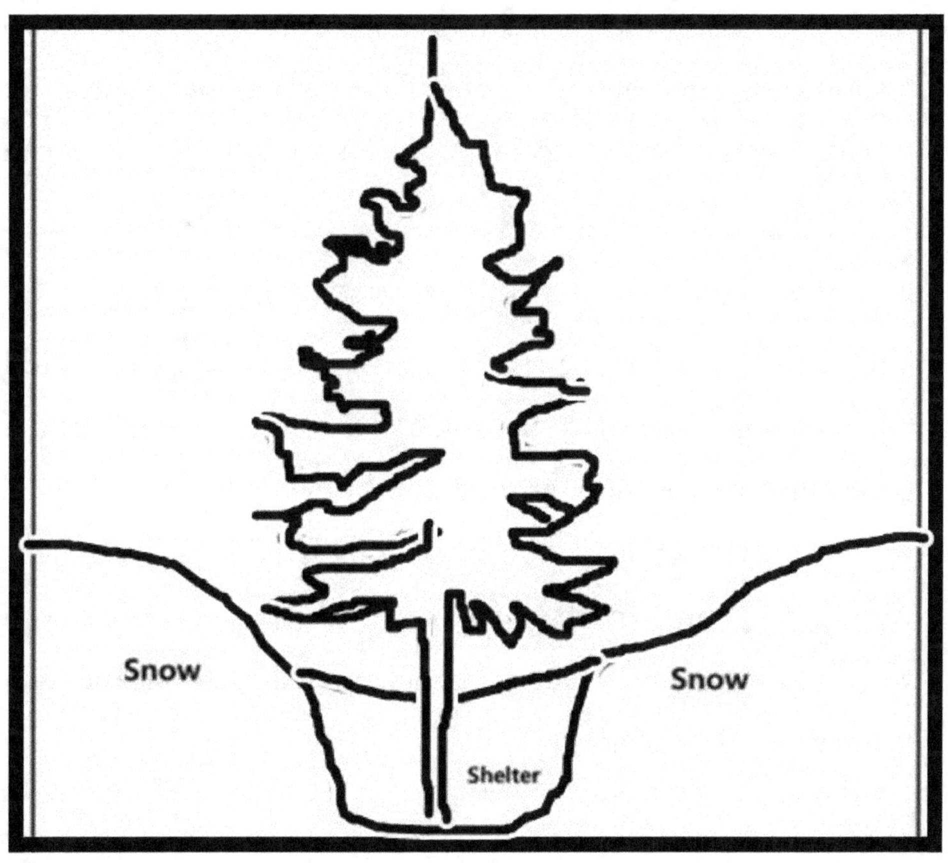

This shelter can only be built if there is a deep layer of snow. However, it can be dug to support several people sitting.

If you have more time to build a shelter, consider building a lean-to with a fire reflector or an A-frame shelter if you cannot build a fire (MacWelch, 2020b). It is best to build your shelter within the tree well of an evergreen tree as this area is more sheltered from the snow. Look to see if there are any trees you can use to assist you in building the shelter. If you have two trees close to each other or a rock face, you can build a lean-to. If you have a single tree with a V-shape wedge, you can construct an A-frame.

Regardless of which you decide to build, start by creating a bough bed. Clear the area of as much snow as possible. Add two long logs or boughs that will make up the two sides of the bed. Aim to have these as long as you or make do with what you have. In the space between the boughs, add smaller boughs with leaves. You want the leaves to be as dry as possible as you will be lying on this under your shelter. Build the thickness up to be about six inches.

Lean-To

Before building your lean-to, consider which direction the snowfall and wind are coming from. You want to construct your wall so that it takes most of the brunt of the weather.

Start with two study branches that have V-shaped notches in them. These branches will be keeping your horizontal ridgeline in place against the trees. You can knock in wooden stakes to keep these branches in place.

Now you have your frame. Get branches to cover one side of the wall. Pack them as tightly together as possible.

Continue to add branches with leaves to add another layer to the wall. Continue to do this until you can't see through to the other side.

Move onto constructing walls to cover the gaps formed between the frame and the tree. Follow the same instructions as you did with the main wall.

The only gap that should remain open is the entrance of your shelter.

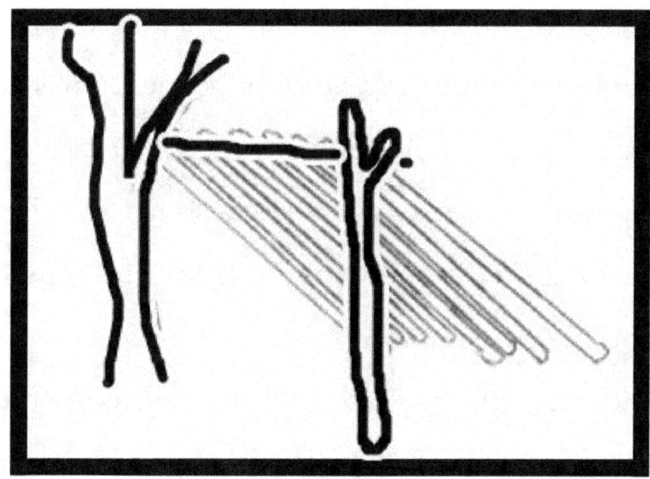

To increase the warmth of the area, build a fire between your shelter and a fire reflector. Alternatively, if you couldn't find dry material for your bough bed, add your emergency blanket. You can fold it double and sleep inside the silver lining. Aim to build the frame long enough for you to rest as comfortable as possible.

A-Frame

This shelter is perfect for keeping you warm if you have no fire. This shelter is generally only big enough for one but can be constructed for two. The smaller the shelter, the easier it will be to keep it warm (McGroarty, 2013).

Find a sturdy branch that is a little longer than what you are. This will be your ridgeline.

Wedge this into the V-shape of a tree and make sure that it cannot be moved. If your ridgeline comes down, so will your entire shelter. Alternatively, you can place one point of the ridgeline between two branches that end in a V-shape. These branches will support the ridgeline and must be buried into the ground to ensure they remain stable.

Once the ridgeline is stable, start by constructing the walls on either side of it. Start by leaning branches from the lowest point of the frame to the highest. Construct walls that are only a little longer than what you are. Don't waste your energy on making something too big to keep warm.

Once these branches are closely packed to each other, start on the next layer.

Collect branches with leaves and create several layers until you can no longer see the inside of the shelter.

Add several layers of leaves or pine needles to add another insulating layer.

Have some spare boughs with dense leaves at the entrance, which you can use to create a door to keep the heat in. Do not seal completely.

If you are concerned about being smothered, omit to seal the bottom of the A-Frame. This way, you still get fresh air if you close the entrance of the shelter.

Be wary of sealing the entrance completely, as there is a chance of more snowfall. This can block the fresh air from entering the bottom of the shelter.

There are various ways to construct these two shelters to make them more weather-friendly, especially if it rains.

Rain Shelter

Getting wet is a danger when you are lost in the woods. This can contribute to you getting hypothermia rapidly. Although the A-frame and lean-to shelters can protect you from rain if you add enough layers, there is always a chance that you can still get wet. If you want to avoid this happening, you can use a waterproof tarp or your emergency blanket as your first layer that goes over or against the ridgeline before adding the branches and twigs (Survival Lily, 2020 & Vuković, 2020). Even if your shelter starts to drip, it will run off of the protective layer.

Pleasant Weather Shelter

Even if the weather isn't extreme, it is a good idea to ensure you have some kind of shelter. Not only will this protect you, but it will also make you feel a little safer, especially if you have a fire going. You can't remain awake constantly and will need to get some sleep at some point. Although there are many single-man shelters that you can put together, only a few of them require next to no equipment. This includes the lean-to made with an emergency blanket or the debris hut (also known as the cocoon form) (Sullivan, 2019).

Debris Hut

No equipment is needed for this shelter. However, this shelter can only insulate you up to a point and will not keep you waterproof.

Clear an area where you want to rest.
Add a layer of branches with leaves to keep you off of the ground.
Start to pile on as many dry leaves as possible. You want to build a mound of about 24–36 inches high and a little longer than what you are.
When you are ready to rest, just wriggle inside.

Although easy to construct, this shelter shouldn't be made too close to a fire, as it is dangerous to catch life. There is also a chance of the leaf litter containing biting creepy crawlies. However, it is the perfect shelter to make when you have run out of daylight to construct a better shelter.

Conclusion

It is human nature to want to provide for our family without relying on anyone or anything outside of ourselves. You will learn that no one will help you when you need it most unless they are truly self-sufficient themselves. This is why becoming more self-reliant is so important to most people. You have to have the mindset that if something happens to the infrastructure of society, then there is no one coming to our rescue. We all have to be prepared with the necessary skills and tools to survive whatever is thrown at us.